THE THIRD WORLD

AFRICA

THE THIRD WORLD SERIES

 AFRICA

 LATIN AMERICA

 MIDDLE EAST

 SOUTH ASIA

 SOUTHEAST ASIA

THE THIRD WORLD

AFRICA

David Wiley
Marylee Crofts

The Dushkin Publishing Group, Inc.
Guilford, Connecticut 06437

Library of Congress Catalog Card Number: 84-93315
Manufactured in the United States of America

First Printing

CONTENTS

AFRICA

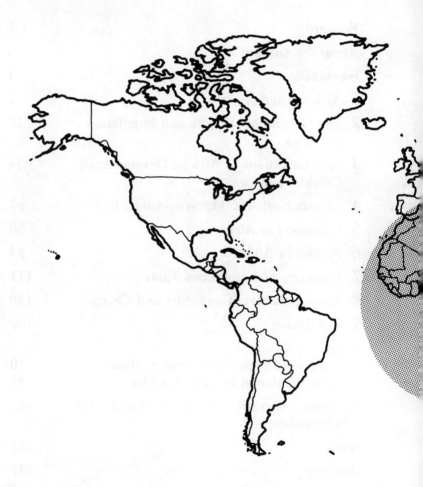

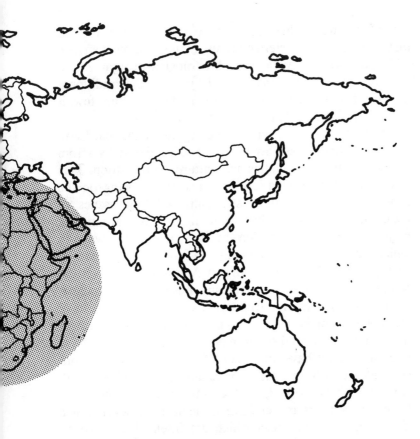

FOREWORD

THE THIRD WORLD has been written to provide much needed materials on non-Western cultures. In the past, most studies of the non-Western world were chronological in organization or dealt with the regions studied by using the traditional themes of religion, politics, history, and so on. Very few, if any, offered the student a thematic perspective.

THE THIRD WORLD discusses the regions of Africa, Latin America, Middle East, South Asia, and Southeast Asia from the perspective of societies and cultures in transition. This has been done in a variety of ways: by focusing on the problems of new nations struggling with the issues of economic development; by organizing the study around the major minorities of a region; by investigating the ways in which traditional norms and modern forms interact; and by seeing the problems of modern non-American cultures in the light of the anxieties, conflicts, and tensions of our society.

In their own ways, the authors of each of the volumes have attempted to make their regions come alive. The authors teach subjects related to the region about which they have written, and all have spent considerable time there. Consequently, they have a deep appreciation for the peoples with whom they have worked, and the cultures in which they have lived. The authors are sensitive to the need for developing a knowledge of their areas which are intelligible to young Americans, but which, at the same time, are region-centric rather than Euro- or America-centric. The significance of such a perspective is illustrated by two plaques on a nineteenth century Spanish monument on the island of Mactan in the

Philippines glorifying God, Spain, the Queen Regent then in power, and Ferdinand Magellan. In 1941 a historical marker titled, "Ferdinand Magellan's Death" was anchored into the monument stating, "On this spot Ferdinand Magellan died on April 27, 1521, wounded in an encounter with the soldiers of Lapulapu, Chief of Mactan island. One of Magellan's ships, the Victoria, under the command of Juan Sebastian Elcano, sailed from Cebu on May 1, 1521, and anchored at San Lucar de Barrameda on September 6, 1522, thus completing the first circumnavigation of the earth." Ten years later, in 1951, the newly independent Republic of the Philippines erected a second marker entitled "Lapulapu." It read, "Here, on 27 April 1521, Lapulapu and his men repulsed the Spanish invaders, killing their leader Ferdinand Magellan. Thus, Lapulapu became the first Filipino to have repelled European aggression."

The authors of the volumes of THE THIRD WORLD are not only interested in these countries from an academic point of view. They also hope to be able to make a contribution to world understanding and world peace by increasing your knowledge of non-Western cultures, peoples, and societies.

THE THIRD WORLD has, in short, been written with a sense of urgency and a sense of mission. The urgency is the chaotic state of today's world. The mission is knowledge, not the kind of knowledge that comes from memorizing facts, but the understanding that comes from dispelling myths and from grappling with problems relevant to you and the world in which you live. You have a stake in the future of the world. It's a rapidly shrinking world in which the problems of the Third World are your problems. It's up to you to try to solve them. We hope that THE THIRD WORLD will be of some help along the way.

—**Donald K. Swearer**
Editorial Advisor
Third World Series
Swathmore College

ABOUT THE AUTHORS

David Wiley is Associate Professor of Sociology and Director of the African Studies Center at Michigan State University. Born in southern Illinois, Mr. Wiley attended Wabash College and Yale University Divinity School. In 1961, he worked for two years in Salisbury, Rhodesia (now Zimbabwe), in the field of race relations. After completing a doctorate in sociology and sociology of religion, he returned to Zambia (formerly Northern Rhodesia) where he conducted research on social stratification and religious organizations in Lusaka, as well as an investigation into the sociology of economic change. He serves on the United States National Commission for UNESCO and on the Committee for World Sociology of the American Sociological Association.

Born in South Bend, Indiana, Marylee Crofts pursued her education at Hanover College where, in 1958, she graduated *magna cum laude* with a degree in Modern Languages. She earned an M.A. degree in French at the University of Wisconsin. Ms. Crofts was an American Field Service exchange student to Germany in 1953, and participated in international work camps from 1957-1962, in Europe, Latin America, and Africa. She has taught school in Zambia and Zimbabwe and in the United States at Michigan State University.

Both authors have been active in organizations supporting the liberation of Southern Africa from racial domination.

INTRODUCTION

This survey of African society has been written primarily for Americans who have had no prior contact with Africa. It is too brief to encompass the rich complexity of contemporary Africa, but attempts to whet the student's appetite for further study.

Recent scholarship reveals the extensive impact African cultures have had on the development of American values and arts. It is our hope that this work will contribute to an increased American understanding of that continent which, due to ignorance, has remained the "dark continent" for too long.

We wish to thank all of those who assisted us by reading early drafts of this book, especially Katherine Thuermer. Most of all, however, we wish to thank those many African friends and acquaintances who opened their homes and communities to us, enabling us to learn from their rich heritage and from the genius of their societies.

1

AFRICANS AND AMERICANS

When you know who his friends are, you know who he is.

Senegalese Proverb

Africans and Americans have been in direct contact for more than two hundred years. Indeed, at the time of the American Revolution in 1776, one American in five had come from Africa. Today the average African-American family in the United States has roots going back two hundred years, whereas the average European-American family's roots go back only one hundred years. Much of what we think of as American music, speech, style, cuisine, and art has originated in or been heavily influenced by the African origins of so many Americans.

For more than two hundred years, the exchange between Africa and America has been primarily commercial—with many Americans hoping to profit from the bountiful African resources. The first profiteers were the Yankee merchants who sailed their clipper ships around Africa to buy spices from the Orient. Later, American merchant shipment transported thousands of African slaves from their homelands to the plantations of the Americas. Yankee whalers, too, sailed into African ports for provisions and trade. As a result of this trade and the need for diplomatic protection along African coasts, the first American government contacts were in South Africa, where a consulate was established in 1799. The United States was even tempted to annex territory on that coast in the early nineteenth century.

Recent exchanges between the United States and Africa have been more friendly. We have sent teachers and medical, agricultural, and technical personnel in response to needs of African nations. These people were sent through Christian missions, the Peace Corps, and private and government aid plans. Many African leaders have been educated in the United States since the 1940s. Throughout this mixed history of exploitation and friendship, Africans and Americans have gained in several ways from one another.

FROM AFRICA TO AMERICA

The peoples of Africa brought their rich cultural heritage to the New World. African proverbs, aphorisms, and folk tales were told across the southern plantations and found their way into the oral and written literature of Americans. Best known among these are the tales about that famous African trickster, Br'er Rabbit and the other tales of Uncle Remus. African languages, too, had their impact on American, Greek, Finnish, or French origin of the term "OK," a noted linguist has traced that favorite Americanism to a term used in West Africa among the Wolof and Mandingo peoples. Indeed, it is estimated that over eighty American expressions probably have an African origin.

Even more well-known are the African beginnings of Afro-American music, known to us through the blues, ragtime, jazz, soul, and reggae music. On the plantations and in the cities of the slave South, the many Afro-American traditions of dance and song were kept alive in the nineteenth century. Later they were popularized by the professional black music of the twentieth century. By the mid-twentieth century, the importance of African musical contributions to America was well-recognized; some American musicians such as Duke Ellington and Louis Armstrong traveled to Africa to draw directly on African rhythms and melodies.

Stan Kenton, another innovator in American music, actually copied various African drum rhythms in jazz recordings in the 1950s.

More indirectly, African art has had a significant influence on drawing and painting styles in Europe and America. Pablo Picasso, Amedeo Modigliani, and other European expressionist and impressionist artists were influenced by the African mask as an art form. Some of the faces in their paintings are virtual replicas of masks of West Africa. African figure caricature, with its flattened images of human bodies and of animals, can be seen in such movie and television cartoons as the Pink Panther, Road Runner, and various Disney productions.

The very presence of black Americans in this country has enriched the whole social fabric. This country owes much of its power and material wealth to both the labor of the African slaves brought here to work on the plantations and to the pool of cheap immigrant and black labor on which American urban and industrial development was founded. Even though at the time of the American Revolution so many Americans were the sons and daughters of Africa, they have not shared in the full benefits of the economic productivity that they helped to create. For almost two centuries, white Americans have enjoyed a high standard of living partly because the descendants of African peoples received so little for their work.

Just as economically important have been the raw materials brought from Africa for American industry and consumer products. Although the chocolate bar is an American institution, most American chocolate is of African origin, primarily a product of the farmers of the Ivory Coast and Ghana. Cola, used in soft drinks, is extracted from West African cola nuts. Coconut oils for soaps, cloves, sisal for rope and sacking, sugar, tea, coffee, and other products come from Africa. American jets, missiles, and lunar modules are constructed with high-grade chrome from Zimbabwe and

South Africa. Nigeria is the second-largest foreign supplier of high-grade crude petroleum oil to the United States. Because of its interest in the United States, Nigeria kept American industries working during the oil embargo in the 1970s. Angola, Libya, and Algeria also provide the United States with petroleum and natural gas. Vanadium and manganese originate from Ghana, and columbium comes from Zaire and Niger. We repel mosquitos with Kenyan pyrethrum. America's first atomic bombs were manufactured with Zairean uranium. Even the American cowboy had an earlier African origin. Cattle, horses, and cattle-ranching methods were brought to the Americas by the Spanish, who learned cattle-ranching techniques from the Moors of North Africa.

Americans and West Europeans have had the advantages of less expensive autos, airplanes, and other consumer products because Africans are paid low wages to produce these essential materials: rubber, iron ore, chrome, copper, industrial diamonds, bauxite, oils, and petroleum.

Africa continues to provide a growing number of American industries with new markets, and American investors are making new profits there. Across the African continent are found Hilton Hotels and Holiday Inns; Chrysler, Ford, and General Motors autos; Boeing and Lockheed planes; Gulf, Mobil, and Texaco petroleum; IBM computers; Kodak and Polaroid cameras and film; and hundreds of other American products and firms. The more Africa develops, the more these companies will find a ready market for their goods and services.

FROM AMERICA TO AFRICA

Americans have been an important source of education for African nations—first through missionaries and their schools and then through the Peace Corps and other volunteers. Because America was not a colonial power in Africa, the local peoples came to American missions with fewer suspicions. Some missions even planted the seeds of opposition to the colonial powers—both in their message of religious freedom, which had political consequences, and in their opposition to some of the practices of the companies and the colonial governments.

Africans came to American schools and universities as early as the mid-nineteenth century. A number of famous African leaders who fought for independence got their first taste of freedom from colonial rule as students in America. These included Nnamdi Azikiwe of Nigeria, Tom Mboya of Kenya, Hastings Banda of Malawi, and Kwame Nkrumah of Ghana. Since then, hundreds more Africans have come to American campuses for graduate training in science, arts, administration, and technology. Yet, even before these leaders emerged, American blacks had been a source of revolutionary new ideas for black independence and black unity. The first "back to Africa" movement in 1847, when almost twelve thousand African-Americans returned to West Africa, produced the independent nation of Liberia. Later, in the 1850s, other black Americans made journeys to Nigeria and (after 1900) to Ethiopia to arrange for many Afro-Americans to return to Africa. Very few of those who considered immigration actually returned because they were faced with high transportation costs and an uncertain future in Africa.

From 1880 to 1925, many writings about African self-determination, African personality, and black pride flowed back and forth across the Atlantic in the works of Bishop Henry M. Turner, W.E.B. DuBois, and Marcus Garvey. So important were these ideas of freedom to Africans in their growing consciousness of their exploitation that a number of colonial powers in West and South Africa sought to ban "dangerous" black Americans from their shores.

In the 1920s, the New York "Harlem Renaissance" sparked even greater popular pride in black culture and black accomplishments. The themes of this movement were embraced by African and Caribbean writers, including Leopold Senghor of Senegal and Aimé Césaire. These two prophets of black pride originated the concept of "Negritude." Simultaneously, black American churchmen were increasingly interested in the African foundations of Christianity including the flight of the holy family (Joseph, Mary, and Jesus) into Egypt; Simon of Cyrene, the first African cross-bearer; the Eunuch of Ethiopia; the theology of Augustine, a North African bishop; and the "oldest Christian nation," Ethiopia. This new interest was reflected in the writings and sermons of black churchmen and even in the names of churches, such as the Abyssinian (Ethiopian) Baptist Church and the African Methodist Episcopal Church. Some black Americans found a special calling working as missionaries in Africa. In the 1930s, a number of black Americans went to Ethiopia to help Emperor Haile Selassie develop the nation and defend the territory against the Italian Army. One black American pilot, known as the Brown Condor, was the emperor's personal courier from Addis Ababa to the front lines during the war.

During World War II and the Korean War, the interests of black Americans were absorbed in the American war effort to defeat Germany, Japan, and North Korea. Black Americans and Africans in British and French colonies were drafted in record numbers to fight for the Allies.

By the mid-1950s, however, there was a resurgence in the interest of Africans and Afro-Americans in each other. The nationalist movements in Africa were gaining momentum. The push for freedom resulted in the political independence of dozens of nations between 1958 and 1965. As the diplomats and ambassadors of these newly emancipated countries appeared in Washington and at the United Nations, there was a stirring of black American pride. Some Africans even spoke out against America's segregationist laws and practices. Black Americans appeared in Africa as American

(United Nations photo)

Independence is a cause for celebration in many former colonies. Parades and bands commemorate independence day in Tanzania.

ambassadors, tourists, US Information Agency personnel, and scholars. Malcolm X wrote of black American indebtedness to Africa. Although many Afro-Americans were absorbed in the domestic civil rights and black nationalist struggles of the mid-1960s, some were beginning to take an even greater interest in Africa. The result was a veritable explosion of interest in products of African origin in black communities. The *dashiki* shirt, African cloth for skirts, African mask pendants and home decorations, and African sculpture gained new popularity. More and more Afro-Americans began "pilgrimages" to Africa to discover their pre-slavery roots. African names were being given to some young children, and even the Afro hairstyle was regarded by some as an expression of pride in the natural beauty of black people. Muhammad Ali and Kareem Abdul Jabbar are but two black Americans who have returned to an African religion. American civil rights leader, Stokley Carmichael, married African songstress Miriam Makeba and traveled to Africa to confer with former Ghanaian President Kwame Nkrumah on the means to achieve black liberation in Africa and America.

Politically, black Americans have been increasingly interested in American policy toward Africa. As a result, former Congressman Charles Diggs of Detroit became the first black chairman of the House of Representatives Foreign Affairs Subcommittee on Africa. He was joined by black Congressmen Dellums and Conyers. The Black Congressional Caucus, which included these and other senators and congressmen, was formed in 1971 and began to make demands for the national interests of black Americans. In a Black Manifesto submitted by the caucus to President Richard Nixon in 1971, the members demanded an American policy on South Africa, Zimbabwe, and the Portuguese colonies that was more closely aligned with black rather than with white interests. All through the 1970s and 1980s, these Congressmen and their white colleagues and supporters provided an important lobby against racism in Africa. Thus, Africa may have a new black American constituency for its interests in the same way that Irish-Americans and Jewish-Americans have formed interest groups and lobbies for their "homelands."

After achieving their independence, many African nations looked to the United States as a source of aid and assistance. America was wealthy, had experienced British colonial rule, and had not been a colonial power in Africa. Furthermore, at the United Nations and in Africa, Americans declared their firm support for African self-determination, their commitment to a decade of development in the 1960s, and their opposition to white domination in Southern Africa. As a result, Americans found a warm welcome in Africa in the early 1960s. Peace Corps volunteers and other Americans seemed to identify easily with Africans and their newly won independence. Loans and some American foreign aid were sent to African nations. Thus, the 1960s was an era of "good feeling" between most Americans and Africans.

NEW QUESTIONS FROM AFRICANS
TO AMERICANS

In the 1970s and 1980s, however, many African leaders increasingly began to question American intentions in Africa. "Do you really support us and our self-determination in action as well as in words?" they have asked. The basic question being posed by these black nations is whether or not the world's most powerful nation will continue to lend its support and growing economic power to South Africa, the last society in the world still officially operating on a legalized racism. Africans firmly believe that the United States has the capacity to act against South African racism instead of supporting it. They are not asking Americans to perfect their own racial situation before considering Africa. acknowledging that both themselves and the United States must work on both problems. As Zambian President Kaunda noted in 1969:

> None of us would claim that within our own States we have achieved that perfect social, economic, and political organization which would insure a reasonable standard of living for all our people and establish individual security against hardship or miscarriage of justice. On the contrary, we acknowledge that within our own States the struggle towards human brotherhood and unchallenged human dignity is only beginning. It is on the basis of our commitment to human equality and human dignity, not on the basis of achieved perfection, that we take our stand of hostility towards the colonialism and racial discrimination which is being practiced in Southern Africa.[1]

As Africans work diligently to raise their standards of living and quality of life, and to gain their freedom from minority rule, the economic and political gap between Americans and Africans may grow. President Julius Nyerere of Tanzania explained why:

> The significant thing about the division between rich and poor nations is not simply that one has the resources to provide comfort for all its citizens, and the other cannot provide basic services. The reality and depth of the problem arises because the man who is rich has power over the lives of those who are poor, and the rich nation has power over the policies of those who are not rich. And, even more important, is that our social and economic system, nationally and internationally, supports these divisions and constantly increases them, so that the rich get ever richer and the more powerful, while the poor get relatively even poorer and less able to control their own future.[2]

Because of the official American position of commitment to democracy, justice, the rule of law, and human welfare, African leaders expect more from the United States government and American citizens than they have been receiving. As Zambian President Kaunda told a group of Americans visiting Africa,

> We ... need the sympathy and understanding of the American people and the people of the world in our search for the best road to economic and social advancement. We are partners in building peace and security in the world. The partnership involving a two-hundred-year-old America rich and full of experience, with a ten-year-old continent of Africa, no doubt demands a lot from the older. But this is natural in many African customs. For in many of our villages, the strong must always help defend the weak. Similarly, in our world community, the strong, the well-endowed, must be ready to assist the weak in order that the entire community can move forward, matching its aspirations on every turning in peace and freedom.[3]

QUESTIONING THE IMAGE OF AFRICA IN AMERICA

He who never visits thinks his mother is the only cook!
                    Ugandan and Ethiopian proverb

Our media present a stereotyped image of Africa—whether it is in television adventure series, in famous old films such as *King Solomon's Mines* and *The African Queen,* or even in our most widely-read newspapers. Often these images distort the reality and complexity of Africa. Various pictures and stories present Africa as a place inhabited by strange "natives" with exotic and primitive ways of life. More recently, we hear of "ravaging tribal conflicts." Few people have access to reliable information about other aspects of Africa, about the real problems and accomplishments of these nations, or about the rich heritage

(United Nations photo)

Among the myths Americans hold about Africa and Africans is this stereotype of the African family. Today, a significant percentage of Africans live in urban areas.

of African social relations. In short, for many Americans Africa is the *Dark Continent.*

Not only do most Americans have little opportunity to learn accurate information, but what we do learn from films, television, videogames, books, and news magazines is often very distorted, biased, and negative.

Most of these images come from television, which even in the 1980s broadcasts many hours of *Tarzan* and animal programs such as *Wild Kingdom* and *Animal World.* Today, more Americans may think of Africa in terms of jungles, animals, and savages than before, when the media was less powerful. Africans are portrayed as savage jungle warriors by amusement and theme park owners, who wish to draw crowds of tourists to see or "experience" the dangers of these exotic people. At Disney parks, "dangerous" plastic warriors rise out of the grass to feint a spear throw at customers, who already are entranced with the snapping alligator or trumpeting elephant. Our fascination with images of strange dress, behavior, or danger—as well as with wild animals—is a ready source of ticket sales and advertising profits.

Africa is different from North America in climate, geographical features, flora and fauna, and customs and cultures. Africans also have many customs and aspects of life in common with Americans. Both have the basic human needs of food, shelter, clothing, education, and good health. Africans and Americans have the same desire for freedom of speech, expression, movement, and religion. Parents on both continents worry about the safety of their children. Like American parents, Africans often fret about the new tastes and styles of young people, who seem to prefer the new, rather than the old, ways. In both societies, there is festival and fun surrounding the occasions of marriages, births, graduations, and promotions at work. The elders of both societies enjoy remembering "the good old days," and families in both continents worry about how they can provide for the needs of the elderly when they are no longer healthy and productive. Americans and Africans spend their days in much the same way—working, preparing food, eating together as families, and traveling to and from work. Although techniques and technology vary in both societies, farmers of both continents plant, weed, and harvest their corn (called maize in Africa) and tend their cattle. Both cattle and corn are the most common products in both continents. When farmers meet, they talk of weather, potential drought, crop yields, problems of insects and disease, the follies and foibles of people in the cities, the pros and cons of different farming techniques, and how to find the best deal from local shops and companies.

Frequently, the African and other non-Western nations which have few skyscrapers, highways, automobiles, medical and technical achievements, and other artifacts of Western material culture are labeled backward, uncivilized, or primitive. By Western material standards, they have failed to progress and to achieve a high level of civilization. In this book, a Western yardstick will not be used to measure the value of African civilization. Instead, we will explore reasons why some types of material culture did not develop in Africa while other aspects of human culture developed more extensively than in the West. African accomplishments in law, social structure, healing arts, and agriculture will be reviewed, as will areas in which African development has been extensive.

At the outset, however, we must first set aside some of the Western myths about African geography and people. Africans and Americans must begin to understand each other, to find common ground, and to explore the common heritage and the global futures that bind them together for all times.

2

THE GEOGRAPHY, WEALTH, AND POPULATION OF AFRICA

Our images of Africa are contradictory—starving babies in crowded refugee camps and piles of gold bullion in South Africa. Africa is, generally, poor—poor in land and production—except in those few places where fantastic mineral wealth has been unearthed: copper in the Shaba Province of Zaïre and Zambia; oil in Nigeria and Libya; and gold, chrome, and uranium in Zimbabwe, South Africa, and Namibia. The gold, diamonds, copper, tin, chromium, oil, coal, and many other resources are essential to Western industry as well as for African development.

In absolute terms, Africa is poor. The average national income per person is less than $8 per week or $411 per year. Africa, with over fifty nations, has only about five percent of the total world trade, but its population is larger than the United States. A large proportion of this trade provides profits for the whites of South Africa and the stockholders of large American, British, and other foreign companies. The total Gross National Product for all of Africa constitutes less than two percent of the world's total. Africa's literacy rate is twenty-eight percent as compared to a world average of over sixty percent. The average life span for an African is forty-seven years; the industrial nations' average is seventy-four years. While there is one doctor for every 620 people in the industrialized nations, Africa has one doctor for every twenty-four thousand people. Africa has the highest death rate and shortest lifespan of all the world's continents.

Africans know they are poor in comparison to Americans or Europeans. All across the continent they have seen health, wealth, and security in the white mission stations, schools, mines, and towns. This so-called "demonstration effect" has made a significant impact on both villagers and townsmen. Freedom from hunger, disease, and insecurity were possible—for a few. The result has been what one sociologist called "the most successful religion in the history of the world," which is the belief in the desirability of material progress, development, health, and security.

We begin this survey of contemporary African society and culture with a discussion of the economy because so much of what occurs in African politics, religion, education, art, and culture depends on the economy. Across Africa today, one fact binds together the diverse peoples—the aspiration for rapid economic development. The general failure to achieve rapid economic change means that Africa in the 1980s is full of increasingly frustrated people, impatient for a better life which they know already exists for Americans, Englishmen, other Europeans, and some elite Africans. To understand why Africa is generally poor, we must survey the sources of African food, work, and production, the population growth, and the health situation.

MYTHS AND REALITIES OF LAND AND CLIMATE

Contrary to popular belief, Africa has varied terrain and climate, ranging from the hot and barren territory of the Sahara and Kalahari deserts to the snowcapped peaks in East Africa. The most common type of land in Africa is the rolling plain, called the savannah or grassland. It is similar to the plains and rolling hills of Indiana and Illinois. The tropical jungle, which Americans came to know in *The African Queen* and the Tarzan films, exists only in a few African countries near the coast and in rain forest areas. (In fact, the makers of early Tarzan movies actually built a

(United Nations photo/G. Tortoli)

The economies of African nations vary according to climate and available resources. In Liberia, rice is an important staple.

jungle set in a park in Uganda to create a movie that would meet American expectations of how Africa should look.) Many Africans have never seen a palm tree, a lion, or an elephant. While outsiders may think of Africa as a place of dampness, moss, mold, and slimy lagoons, many African peoples actually live for long periods each year without rain or in a condition of drought.

The economies of Africa are adapted to the physical potential of the continent's land, minerals, and climate. The extremes in land and climate can make life harsh for those trying to make a living in Africa. Two of the world's great mountains, Mount Kenya and Mount Kilimanjaro, lie near the equator. Both are snow-capped, with cool coffee-growing areas on their lower slopes. The cool, high climates of East, Central, and Southern Africa—from Kenya to South Africa—attracted the white settlers from Europe. These immigrants found a healthy climate and good land. They created large plantations using cheap African farm labor. On the West African coast and in the interior, on the other hand—from Guinea to Zaïre—is the verdant tropical belt with thick swampland and tropical forest areas. This area did not attract white settlement. The climate was unpleasant, and the mosquitos carried malaria and yellow fever. Most white visitors during the nineteenth century had a life expectancy of about one year. Kwame Nkrumah, the first leader of Ghana, wryly noted that a monument should be built to the mosquitos that protected his homeland in West Africa from white settlement.

The heavy rainfall and humidity in that part of Africa causes rapid rust, decay, and mold. Ants and termites that attack any wooden building or furniture abound. New nations in these areas have high building costs because mortar and steel must be widely used. Heavy rainfall spoils stored crops, reducing both the amount of food available and the cash return for the farmer. In torrential rains, the built-up soil can be eroded away in a few hours. Heavy rains also

Table 1
COMPARISONS OF SOCIETIES AND ECONOMIES OF AFRICA AND THE INDUSTRIALIZED NATIONS (PRIMARILY NORTH AMERICA, JAPAN, AND EUROPE), 1979-1981

	Sub-Saharan Africa	Industrialized Countries
Total population	344 million	671 million
Life expectancy at birth	47 years	74 years
Gross National Product (GNP) per person	$411	$9,440
% Increase of GNP per person per year from 1960 to 1979	1.6%	4.0%
Percentage of adults literate	28%	99%
Energy consumption per capita (kilograms of coal equivalent)	128 kg.	7,892 kg.
Crude birth rate per 1,000 population	48 births	15 births
Crude death rate per 1,000 population	18 deaths	10 deaths
Percent of total population living in cities	21%	77%
Number of persons per physician	24,000	620
Daily food calorie supply as a percentage of the needed requirement	89%	131%
Percent of age group enrolled in primary school	63%	100%
Percent of age group enrolled in secondary school	13%	89%
Percent of age 20-24 population enrolled in university	1%	37%
Percent of national budget spent on education	16%	11%
Percent of national budget spent on general public services	22%	8%
Military expenditure as a percent of GNP	3%	3%
Armed forces per 1,000 population	3	7

Source: World Bank, *Accelerated Development in Sub-Saharan Africa*, Washington, 1981.

cause flooding and pooling of water in low areas. This causes poor drainage, bacterial accumulation, and mosquito breeding. Roads are difficult to build and to maintain on the soft, water-logged earth.

Another result of this tropical climate is the low level of protein in the diet. Few beef cattle can survive the heat, humidity, and the tsetse flies that afflict many parts of the tropics. The inhabitants of some of these coastal areas, which account for forty percent of Africa's population, suffer from low protein diets, and they are ill-equipped to withstand the disease and climatic rigors of their homelands.

Life in the central interior is just as rigorous. The typical African countryside is a rolling plain, with high grasses and occasional scrub trees. This land, part of Africa's high (three to six thousand foot) central plateau, stretches the length of the continent. Typically, this area has few major forests because of the shortage of water. Annual rainfall averages thirty to forty inches, but the rains come suddenly in short, torrential downpours during a five- to six-month period. This rain drains rapidly from the land to the rivers, creating erosion in some places. The permanent water table beneath the soil is low because the surface water runs off and does not penetrate the soil. After the rainy season, the dry season comes, frequently leaving the land without even a drop of rain for six to seven months. During this period, the soil becomes dry dust. Dehydration stops the decomposition of vegetation waste needed to build rich soil humus, and dust storms also blow away the topsoil.

Even these extreme wet and dry seasons are not always predictable from year to year. After five good years, there may be one year with virtually no rainfall. This is devastating to farmers. Even during a good year, most food is eaten before the next year's crop is harvested because of food storage problems and the delicate land-to-people balance. A year of low rainfall, then, is a year of hunger. Livestock normally kept for breeding purposes may be slaughtered to feed the human population and because there is no pasture for them. The dryness leaves the savannah parched and subject to huge, rolling prairie fires.

To cope with the poor land, Africans practiced patterns of crop rotation and brush burning called "shifting agriculture." Ashes from the burned brush provided needed minerals and fertilizers for an adequate food crop. But after several plantings, the land was exhausted. It then needed to lie fallow for several years. Thus, a village would shift from plot to plot, maintaining the land as long as possible, then moving to a new site, perhaps several miles distant, where the land had not been worked.

In recent years, urban Africans and the overall growth of the population have exerted great pressure for increased food production. During the colonial period, heavy taxation required by the governments increased the pressure for production of crops to sell for cash which farmers then used to pay their taxes. As a result, the delicate land-to-people ratio was destroyed in many places in Africa, and more hunger has resulted.

Many African societies also tended to place great emphasis on the equality of people, so that even the chief was hungry when others had little to eat. When the chief ate well, the whole society ate well. Usually, the chief did not hoard great surpluses of wealth as did the kings of the ancient civilizations of Egypt, Persia, Greece, Rome, and medieval Europe. Such surpluses of wealth and power for the elite of these famous societies caused great poverty and hunger among the common people. Inequalities did exist, however, in Africa, in kingdoms such as Songhai, Mali, or Bornu where rulers enjoyed inordinate wealth. It is interesting that Westerners frequently point to these kingdoms and their material wealth as great achievements in African history. These kingdoms, however, are important exceptions to the more common egalitarian societies.

The pattern of low annual rainfall, brief torrential rain, and long dry periods accompanied by dust storms, which are typical for many African nations, has made life hard for subsistence farmers. As a result, the new nations of Africa have placed a high priority on building new lakes and reservoirs to store water for use in the dry season. Many modern nations of Africa must develop irrigation systems for better agricultural production, just as many ancient African societies did.

The land mass of Africa rises quickly from the coastal plain and tropical forests up to the plateau. Because of this barrier the interior remained "dark" to early explorers. Phoenician, Portuguese, Arab, and British explorers and traders tried to move inland up the great rivers of Africa, the Congo, the Zambezi, the Volta, and the Orange. Only a few miles inland, they encountered huge unnavigable waterfalls and rapids where the rivers plummet from the high interior plateau. Some people believe that Africa was protected from exploitation and more extensive slave-raiding by these barriers, but today, they prevent efficient and profitable river transport. Now goods must be shipped around these falls and rapids by expensive road and railway transportation. These waterfalls, however, produce needed hydroelectric power.

A second obstacle to the penetration of Africa has been the lack of harbors. The smooth coastline has few usable ports where ships may anchor. The best port, Capetown, is in white-dominated South Africa. Overall, relative to the size of its land mass, Africa has fewer harbors than any other continent.

Africa is the inheritor, however, of a profitable geological fault, known as the Great Rift. This prehistoric rending of the earth's surface formed a chain of valleys the length of the continent—from the Gulf of Suez through Ethiopia, Kenya, Tanzania, Zambia, and Malawi. These wide valleys held water and soil and became fertile farmlands. The exposure of the earth's inner rock strata made available many of the industrial minerals and precious metals: chromium, manganese, tin, lead, silver, gold, and diamonds. Yet, the rift, with its mountains and valleys, has also made the construction of railways and roads difficult and expensive.

In size, Africa is more than three times larger than the continental United States. This enormous size hinders African development. For example, this vastness affects Zambia's national income. Zambia relies on copper exports for over ninety percent of its foreign income. Landlocked in Central Africa, the country for years has hauled copper bars by train to seaports. This journey is equivalent to the distance between Kansas City and New York. When the copper reaches the coast, it is placed on ships to travel several thousand miles to European consumers. It is an expensive route from the mine to the buyer.

THE HUMAN RESOURCE: POPULATION

Africa is not overpopulated. In past centuries, the great expanses of Africa were sparsely populated. In an area of fertile land, such as Nigeria or Uganda, larger populations were found. Most of the land, however, was not fertile, which kept the population small. Even today, the continent has approximately one-fourth of the land mass of the world but only one-tenth of the world's population. It has a density of less than ten people per square mile, compared to a world average of twenty-three. Most of the population still depends on subsistence agriculture, and the people live in rural areas—eighty percent in West Africa, ninety percent in East Africa, and fifty to sixty percent in southern Africa. They are scattered across the open countryside, and this creates many economic problems. The costs of mail delivery, electricity and telephone service, school and hospital construction, and transportation are necessarily high. Several African governments have decided they need larger populations living closely together in order to produce more and reduce the cost of services at the same time.

Africa's low population density does not mean the continent does not have population problems. The relatively infertile land, inadequate rainfall, and high disease rate all traditionally cause a short life span and a high infant mortality rate. The population has been in balance with the reesources available, but now the balance has been upset by a number of factors. The movement to urban areas has created new consumers who do not produce food. They depend on the farmers to supply their needs. Another factor is the increasing life span and the decreasing infant mortality rate of Africans. These result from better medical care, and more doctors, nurses, clinics, and hospitals. But Africa is in the midst of a population explosion. New data suggest that the birthrate for the continent of Africa may be the highest in the world and that the death rate is half the birthrate.

The reduction of the rate of infant mortality has brought a new phenomenon to Africa: a very young population. The average age is approximately eighteen years. It is estimated that half of the population of Zaïre is under sixteen years of age. The youthfulness of the population means a greater demand for schools. It also means that there are more people to feed who are too young to work. The high death rate also means that the older generation is replaced more rapidly than in Western nations where elders live longer, thereby preserving older solutions and resisting change. Thus, even the high death rate facilitates rapid social change.

Some experts believe that Africa's population will increase in the next forty years from about 300 million to almost 800 million. Economic development will be hindered by this rapid growth in population. The rate of population growth is 2.7 percent, whereas in the United States the figure is less than one percent. Not only is Africa's growth rate high, but there is evidence that it is rising. This is serious because it is estimated that for every one percent increase in population, an African nation needs a 4.5 percent increase in Gross National Product just to meet the basic human needs.

Thus, as a whole, Africa needs an economic growth rate of over twelve percent (2.7 × 4.5) just to "stay even." Few African countries are achieving at that rate. In the face of this struggle to "stay even," African governments are encountering a "revolution of rising expectations." People demand change now—not tomorrow or in ten years. While the average African may not totally perceive the effects of the population increase, he or she does know when a paycheck buys less or when the promised hospital is not built because funds are lacking. The results of such strains are becoming intolerable.

HEALTH AND WELFARE IN AFRICAN DEVELOPMENT

Social surveys in Africa consistently show a desire for increased health care, hospitals, and trained medical doctors. In spite of the many stories about the continent's supposed resistance to modern medicine, the problem is not that there are too few patients but too many. In twelve African nations, the ratio of doctors to the population is one doctor per twenty thousand people. In Ethiopia, the ratio is one doctor per seventy-five thousand people.

Poor health care means lower life expectancy. It also decreases the number of productive years for African men and women to produce food and income for their families. Poor health care also means less preventive medicine because the doctors and nurses must deal first with emergencies. Prenatal and postnatal care are inadequate. Probably half of all African children die before they reach the age of six. This causes much tragedy in African family life.

Several diseases flourish in Africa's tropical climate, especially malaria, sleeping sickness, river blindness, schistosomiasis, and tuberculosis, but the most basic health problem is malnutrition. Although malaria was traced to the mosquito as early as the 1890s, no adequate cure for the disease has been discovered. Many young Africans contract malaria, suffering occasional attacks of the fever throughout their lives. Sleeping sickness is transmitted by the tsetse fly, which is found in the scrub tree and forest regions of central Africa. It kills cattle, which reduces the already limited protein source in the diet of rural populations. Sleeping sickness also infects and kills humans.

In much of the African savannah, villagers must rely on starchy foods for about eighty percent of their diet. This low vitamin and protein diet means that the people are weaker, more susceptible to new diseases, less energetic and even learn more slowly. While these people can cope with the pace and demands of agricultural labor, the rigors of mining and industrial labor inflict a heavy physical toll.

Parasitic worms, such as in the intestinal hookworm, are another health hazard in Africa. The parasitic bilharzia, for example, begins life in a host snail and infects people as they wade in shallow waters. The bilharzia causes severe injury to the liver. African scientists are seeking ways to destroy the life cycle of this parasite.

Communicable viral and bacterial diseases are developing within Africa's dense urban settlements. The combination of unclean water, poor sanitation, crowded urban living quarters, and poor ventilation encourage the spread of pneumonia, plague, typhus, and other infections.

The cycle of poor health that afficts many people begins with malnutrition and disease in the mother. As a result of the mother's poor, starchy diet, her milk is less nutritious and her baby is more vulnerable to diseases. Many babies do not survive their first year. Another critical period occurs when the baby is weaned. Through nursing, the baby is protected by its mother's immunities. At weaning, the child joins the general population's dependence on starchy foods to ward off illness. Consequently, the death rate after weaning is very high. As a partial solution, many new nations are spending much of their money for varied and nutritious foods—

imported cheese and milk from New Zealand, wheat from
Canada, baby foods from Britain, and fish from Greece. If
African agriculture could provide a more balanced diet, the
money spent on food imports could be spent on other types of
desperately needed development.

AFRICAN SOCIETIES AND AFRICAN ECOLOGY

Historically, six major types of African societies developed
in ancient Africa to cope with the realities of land, population, and climate: hunting and gathering societies; cattle
herding societies; forest dwellers; fishermen; granary societies; and urban societies.

The livelihood of the *hunting and gathering peoples,* or
"societies of the bow," was based on hunting game. When
game was scarce, they relied on roots, herbs, and berries.
Today there are very few such societies; they constitute less
than one percent of the total African population. The Khoi
and San (or Khoisan) peoples of the Kalahari Desert in
southern Africa are well-known examples. The Khoisan
were a short people whose lives depended on hunting. They
lived in bands of about twenty people. The Khoisan developed
their unique and highly successful adaptation to the desert
lands when they were forced out of the fertile savannah by
the migration of other Africans and Europeans. Today few of
the Khoisan people continue to live as their ancestors did.
Most work on farms in Botswana or in mines and industries
in South Africa. ∤

In the African savannah, where there is no tsetse fly, live
the *cattle herding societies.* These groups developed around
the ownership, herding, bartering, and consumption of beef
cattle. Some cattle herding can be found among the Fulani of
Northern Nigeria, the Masai of Kenya, and the Zulu of
South Africa even though many of these people also live in
towns and cities. They created a division of labor: men herd
and hunt while women garden and build homes. Such

societies require large land areas for grazing cattle because of
the sparse grass on the plains. Thus the population, sometimes nomadic, is scattered over wide areas. Since the cattle
may be rustled and driven away (unlike grain and game),
they must develop protection against raiding. Long ago, the
spear and shield were developed for protection and fighting.
The famed nineteenth-century warrior, Shaka, lived among
the South African Zulu, one of the cattle-herding societies.
His armies conquered many people and struck fear into the
hearts of the frontier white populations who wanted the lands
of South Africa.

These societies also produced the age-ranking system by
uniting, through rituals, groups of young boys of the same
age group. These boys would then stay together as they grew
older and took on different positions in their society. They
would first serve as herd boys, then become warriors, and
finally move to positions of governing and teaching in their
middle and older years. This age-rank system provided all
men with a guarantee that even though they must bear the
onerous burdens of herding cattle and fighting against
raiders, they would inherit someday the positions of authority
in society.

The *tropical forests societies* related to nature in a
different way. Because the land was relatively more fertile,
large populations could be supported in these areas. Most
often, the people lived in scattered villages. This scattering
prevented overuse of the land. With iron axes and hoes, these
people cut away the dense brush, piled and burned it, and
used the ash for fertilizer for crops such as *cassava* (a large
tuber which tastes like potatoes when cooked), sweet potatoes, bananas, *plantains* (hard green "bananas" which must
be cooked), and some cereal grains. In these societies
villagers were bound to one another in tightly knit groups
who depended on each other for help. Together they cleared
the dense forest areas, planted, and harvested. In times of
trouble or disease, they assisted one another.

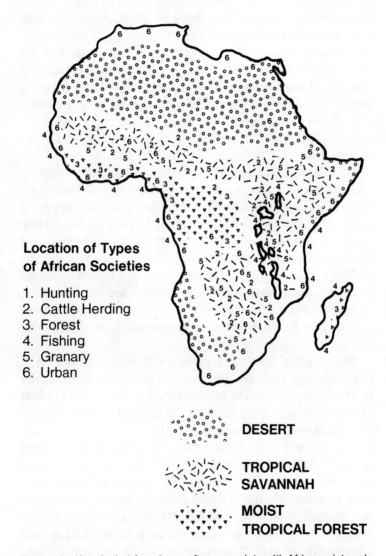

**Location of Types
of African Societies**

1. Hunting
2. Cattle Herding
3. Forest
4. Fishing
5. Granary
6. Urban

DESERT

**TROPICAL
SAVANNAH**

**MOIST
TROPICAL FOREST**

The tropical jungle that Americans often associate with Africa, exists only
in limited regions along the west coast. African societies reflect the terrain
and climate.

On the coasts and along the rivers, the societies of *fishermen* found good sources of protein for their diet. Their life centered around fishing, which was usually done with nets. They traded the fish for animal skins, food, and other necessities from people of the interior forests. Some members of the villages were specialists in boat-building or net-making, but all the work required cooperation. Coastal people lived the uncertain life of the seagoing fishermen. Good nutrition in these areas helped create large and dense populations.

The *granary societies* developed on the open plateau and in the areas infested with the tsetse fly, where cattle could not live. These people used the slash-and-burn technique to clear land in order to grow millet, sorghum, manioc, rice, and maize (corn). These societies, unlike the mobile cattle herders, needed order and stability. They required stable systems of land tenure, guaranteeing each family adequate land for crops. Unlike the tropical coastal societies, surpluses of food occasionally developed in the savannah. These surpluses meant that some of the people could be freed from farming in order to follow specialized crafts of artistry, metalworking, and trade with adjacent societies.

The need for order in the more diversified granary and cattle herding societies encouraged the growth of government and bureaucracy. Laws and codes developed to govern the use of land, and chieftains ruled with their royal clerks, tax-gatherers, police, and priests.

In past centuries the *urban societies* flourished in West Africa along the edge of the forest-savannah transitional area. As early as the first millennium after Christ, an urban area called Jenné-jeno existed in Mali. This city pre-dates the urban centers that developed along with the trade between Arab areas of North Africa and the sub-Saharan area. Successful cattle herding and cereal agriculture supported these societies. Agricultural surpluses created wealth for the urban societies. Trade was possible, and long trade

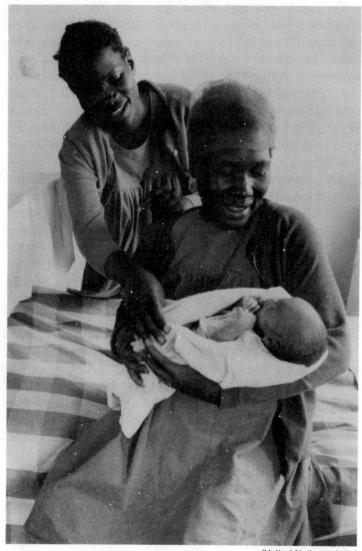

(United Nations photo)

Although settled societies have resulted in improvements such as this maternity ward, population increases put greater pressure on already burdened economies.

routes developed southward into the Congo and northeastward across the Sahara to the Arab societies of the Mediterranean. Leather, ivory, gold, animal skins, feathers, timber, artwork in metals, and other trade goods were sold. Control of taxes, trade, and land required bureaucracies, some of which were patterned after those of the kings of Muslim officials north of the Sahara. The result was the development of the world-famous urban centers in the kingdoms of Ghana, Mali, and Songhai. Today, we find the influence of such West African developments in Kano, Zaria, Ouagadougou, Timbuktu, and in the lakeside and port cities in Central and East Africa.

These six types of societies successfully adapted to difficult conditions of land and climate. Often, two types of societies lived near each other. In such cases, exchange, trade, and tensions could and did develop. For instance, in southern Africa, the breakthrough in military technology of the Zulu people (a cattle society) brought about increased raids and wars, creating turmoil, upheaval, and the migration of many people as far away as East and Central Africa. Similar changes and upheavals occurred in other parts of Africa. Thus, when the first European sailors reached Africa in the late fifteenth century, the continent already was undergoing rapid social, cultural, and technological change. But few men—either black or white—could envision the material, economic, and social change that the European white man would bring to Africa with his slave ship, gun, religion, government, and the instrument of permanent change, the school.

3

NEW DIRECTIONS OF AFRICAN DEVELOPMENT: COLONIES AND NATIONS

Desire for adventure, profit, and land brought whites to Africa in the mid-nineteenth century. The Portuguese export of gold from the Angola-Congo area and tales about a city of gold in Central Africa spurred colonists and companies to seek territory where great wealth might be found. For most, the results were disappointing. The vast distances of Africa and the problems of climate and health defeated the attempts of many colonists to achieve fame and fortune. However, some did find great wealth in farming and mining, utilizing forced and poorly paid African labor. This condition exists in white-ruled South Africa even today.

Slaves for plantation labor were the first commodity shipped from Africa to Europe and the New World. Later, ivory, gold, and palm oil were sought for industrial use and ornament, and soap-making respectively. The end of the slave trade in the early 1900s did not stop the atrocities committed against the peoples of Africa. New forms of exploitation developed: land takeover, taxation without representation, and forced labor migrations. These abuses developed around two whirlpools of turmoil and development: the plantation and the mine.

The coveted legendary wealth of King Solomon's mines was never found by the early explorers. Some sought it in what is now Zimbabwe where Europeans severely damaged the Great Zimbabwe stone structures in their frantic search

FORMER COLONIAL POWERS IN AFRICA

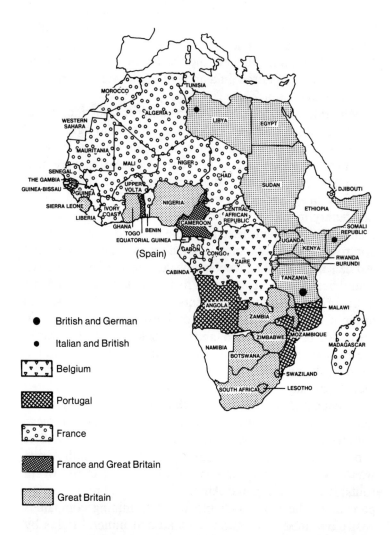

- ● British and German
- • Italian and British
- Belgium
- Portugal
- France
- France and Great Britain
- Great Britain

The European powers competed for the abundant resources of the African continent.

for this gold. Important veins of gold were found in Zimbabwe and South Africa, which already had been mined by
indigenous African peoples. Later, prospectors for the
mining companies discovered most of the currently known
world deposits of diamonds, cobalt, and manganese, as well as
great resources of copper, chrome, vanadium, asbestos, tin,
lead, and uranium. Indeed, the fissionable material for the
atomic bombs of Hiroshima and Nagasaki was mined in the
Shaba Province of Zaïre.

Minerals were the greatest attraction for outside investment in Africa until the 1940s. Only then did agricultural
products begin to displace minerals in importance. Most of
the transportation systems of present-day Africa were built
to transport the wealth produced by the mines. The railroads
and first dirt-gravel roads were used primarily to haul mining
machinery in and to transport the mineral wealth out. (The
colonial governments used the same roads to carry troops for
controlling their colonies.) Some economists claim that
Africa's most significant economic development has occurred
solely because of the export of metals and metal ores. Most
of the private foreign investments in Africa by 1940 were in
the mineral-rich territories of southern Africa. Half was in
the nation of South Africa, and most of the remainder was in
the British colonies. Smaller amounts were invested in the
French, Portuguese, or Belgian areas. Today, the total
income of each African country is very closely correlated
with its amount of mineral wealth and with the investments
made by huge mining corporations. The risks for these
companies seemed great at first, but the profits reaped after
World War II were mammoth. By the 1960s, South Africa
was producing ninety percent of all the gold in the world
(outside the USSR), and African nations had mined eighty
percent of the world's diamonds. The mining companies
easily obtained concessions to land and mineral rights by
manipulating the local peoples. European colonial governments were willing to work closely with these companies

because the colonies were expensive to administer, and company profits could be taxed. Added to the personal taxes paid by Africans, this new income could support the salaries and expenses of the colonial administrators.

Plantation farming first developed in the more tropical areas of West Africa, the Congo (now Zaïre), Angola, and later in East Africa. The Unilever Company of the Belgian Congo controlled almost two million acres. This plantation area is larger than the whole of Belgium, the colonial power. By 1960, this huge company employed fifty thousand Africans, and was producing about $19 million worth of palm oil and other agricultural products per year with only a $64 million investment. The vast Firestone rubber plantations were established in Liberia. Similar ventures were established to produce tea in Malawi and Uganda; fruits in Somalia, Zimbabwe, Cameroon, and the Ivory Coast; sisal in Kenya and Tanzania; and coffee in various countries. In each of these places, the resident African peoples were deprived of the land on which they had lived, farmed, and buried their ancestors. A new source of cash income was established by these monopolistic, conglomerate corporations. The profits, of course, went disproportionately to those who owned and managed the capital, and the European colonial power benefited more than the indigenous peoples. Just before Zaïre, the former Belgian Congo, became independent in 1960, the profits of one of these corporations alone were greater than the entire budget of the colonial government in the former Congo.

The developers of the huge plantations found it difficult to establish crops that would grow, survive, and have a worldwide market. In Kenya, British Lord Delamere struggled for many years to find a strain of wheat that would not die of wheat-rust. When one such crop did succeed, there was a tendency to specialize in that crop. The growing world population and the increasing markets for rubber, tea, coffee, sisal, jute, and sugar also encouraged mass production of

AFRICA

Table 2
THE UNEQUAL ECONOMIES OF AFRICA, UNEQUAL GROWTH, AND SOURCES OF EXPORT EARNINGS

Country or Region	Per Capita Gross National Product, 1979	Average Annual Growth of GNP 1960 to 1979	Leading Exports with % of value of the nation's total exports, 1967
The Wealthy Exporters: GNP per capita over $1,500 per year			
Libya	$8,170	5.8%	Oil 99.8 %
Gabon	3,280	6.1	Oil 30%, Manganese 27%, Timber 25%
South Africa	1,720*	2.3	Gold, 35%
Algeria	1,590	2.4	Petroleum 73%
The Middle Income Nations: GNP per capita at least $400			
Tunisia	1,120	4.8%	Phosphates 30%, Oil 15%
Ivory Coast	1,040	2.4	Coffee 32%, Timber 26%
Mauritius	1,030	2.3	Not available
Botswana	720	9.1	Not available
Nigeria	670	3.7	Petroleum
Swaziland	650	7.2	Not available
Congo	630	0.9	Timber 35%, Diamonds 34%
Cameroon	560	2.5	Cocoa 28%, Coffee 28%
Zambia	500	0.8	Copper 93%
Liberia	500	1.6	Iron Ore 75%
Egypt	480	3.5	Not available
Zimbabwe	470	0.8	Tobacco 20%, Asbestos 5%
Angola	440	−2.1	Not available
Senegal	430	−0.2	Peanuts 66%
Ghana	400	−0.8	Cocoa 69%
The Low Income Nations: GNP per capita at least $250			
Kenya	380	2.7%	Coffee 30%, Tea 14%
Sudan	370	0.6	Cotton 55%
Togo	350	3.6	Phosphates 38%, Cocoa 30%
Lesotho	340	6.0	Not available
Mauritania	320	1.9	Iron Ore 92%
Uganda	290	−0.2	Coffee 54%
Madagascar	290	−0.4	Coffee 32%
Central African Republic	290	0.7	Diamonds 37%
Guinea	280	0.3	Aluminum Ore 63%
Niger	270	−1.3	Peanuts 76%
Zaïre	260	0.7	Copper 60%
Tanzania	260	2.3	Coffee 16%, Cotton 16%
Sierra Leone	250	0.4	Diamonds 65%
Mozambique	250	0.1	Not available

Country or Region	Per Capita Gross National Product, 1979	Average Annual Growth of GNP 1960 to 1979	Leading Exports with % of value of the nation's total exports, 1967
Benin	250	0.6	Palm Oil 21%
Gambia	250	2.6	Peanuts 86%
The Impoverished Nations: GNP per capita below $250			
Malawi	200	2.9	Tea 27%, Tobacco 26%
Rwanda	200	1.5	Coffee 55%
Burundi	180	2.1	Coffee 83%
Upper Volta	180	0.3	Cattle 51%
Guinea-Bissau	170	n.a.	Not available
Mali	140	1.1	Cotton 30%, Cattle 25%
Ethiopia	130	1.3	Coffee 56%
Somalia	est. 120	n.a.	Hides and Skins 42%
Chad	110	−1.4	Cotton 83%

*The per capita income estimates for South Africa are misleading because the average income of whites is approximately ten times that of blacks.

Data Sources: World Bank, *Accelerated Development in Sub-Saharan Africa*, Washington, 1981; and *World Bank Atlas: 1981.*

single crops. During the early years of experimentation there were high investments with no profits. The European investors were eager for a good return on their investments. When the mines and plantations became successful, profits usually were not shared with African workers. Some plantations and mines deliberately sought a policy which discouraged a permanent African labor force. Because there was a high turnover of employees, the Africans (supposedly) would not be separated from their village way of life; they would not desire the European managerial positions; and they would not have the job security necessary to form unions and thus challenge white domination. Low pay, widespread disease, and all-male barracks discouraged a permanent African labor force from forming. In Zimbabwe, even in the mid-1960s, a wage of fourteen cents per day was not uncommon for workers on white-owned farms.

Throughout Africa single cash crop production also increased on individual farms: cocoa in Ghana; beef cattle in Kenya, Zambia, and Botswana; kenaf (a source of fiber for

(United Nations photo)

African nations face difficult choices in their drive toward development.

rope), sugar beets, and maize on the African plateau. The nations with a high Gross National Product (total national income from all sources) are those with large mineral and cash crop income. These products bring in cash from industrialized nations to buy supplies for constructing roads, schools, hospitals, and public buildings.

ONE-CROP ECONOMIES

Colonial influence led to specialization in mining and agriculture, resulting in single commodity economies, sometimes called "monoculture" (one-crop). More than half of Africa's nations depend on one product—grown or mined—for more than fifty percent of their foreign exchange. Libya, with the highest income of all, derives 99.8 percent of its earnings from oil. Zambia's foreign exchange is ninety-three percent copper exports. Mauritania earns ninety-two percent from iron ore. Whenever there is a mine disaster, an

Table 3
AVERAGE GROWTH PER CAPITA PER YEAR OF GROSS NATIONAL PRODUCT (GNP) 1960-79

	Average GNP Per Capita (U.S. $)	Growth 1960-1979
Western Industrial Economies (incl. Japan)	$9,440	4.0
Middle East Oil Exporters	5,470	5.0
Eastern Bloc Nations incl. USSR	4,230	4.3
African Wealth Exporters	3,690	4.2
African Middle-Income Nations	643	2.4
African Low-Income Nations	294	1.3
African Impoverished Nations	159	1.1

Sources: *World Bank Atlas, 1981* and World Bank, *World Development Report, 1981*, Washington, D.C., 1981.

equipment failure, or a surplus in the West, earnings may fall drastically. For instance, when the Vietnam War ended in the 1970s, the United States ended purchases of copper for war industries. As a result, the economies of Zambia and Zaïre fell into a deep depression. But these mineral-rich nations have an advantage due to the growing world need for metals, ores, and oil. The largest market for these minerals is in the Western nations, where they are used in industry. Occasionally, excess stockpiles are dumped on the market by Western nations, increasing the supply and lowering the prices. Fluctuation in prices has caused the national income of some African nations to fall as much as fifty percent over several years, leading to unanticipated depressions and unemployment. On the other hand, when the demand for these resources is high, development results, as it did in the mid-1960s when copper was in great demand.

The agricultural nations, however, are in a worse situation. There has been a general depression in the world prices paid for many African raw commodities since the mid-1950s. At the very time when most African nations were becoming independent, from 1956-1962, the prices paid for Africa's raw materials fell about fifteen percent, but the prices paid for Western manufactured goods rose by about thirty-five percent. In the 1955-1965 period, African nations developed a large trade deficit of approximately $600 million. By the mid-1960s, Africa was being paid relatively less for its products on the world market than any other continent. This was enough to undermine and defeat plans for African development. Nigeria, with one-fifth of the total population of Africa, is a good example. Nigeria was able to increase its production of peanuts significantly from 1954-1962 through better fertilizers, storage, transportation, and, most importantly, the increased hard work of its farmers. Over those eight years, Nigerians succeeded in raising production from 428,000 tons to 513,000 tons (almost twenty percent). However, prices fell, and Nigeria was paid almost $10 million less for the increased crop. Meanwhile, the price of tractors, fertilizer, and equipment needed to produce the peanuts increased almost fifty percent. Since the discovery of oil in Nigeria many experienced farmers have left agriculture for more lucrative work in oil-related employment.

Nigeria's neighboring state, Ghana, supplies most of the chocolate eaten in America. Ghana's cocoa production accounts for sixty-nine percent of its total export earnings. Over the last twenty years, Ghana has had three major problems caused by its heavy dependence on cocoa. First, the market for Ghana's cocoa has been very unstable. In the London Market, as little as $256 per ton was paid for cocoa in one year (1965). Eleven years before (1954), the price had reached $1,575 per ton. Ghana's cocoa prices do not only vary from year to year; they also rise and fall within a given year. For instance, in 1968, the price varied from $1,372 to $767 per ton. This price variation makes it exceedingly difficult for Ghanaian financial planners to make any commitments of funds, knowing that the fluctuating market may destroy profits which were to be used in development projects. A second problem is that Ghana has lost a large portion of its cocoa trees in windstorms or as a result of a serious root disease. Third, because prices have been low, twenty percent of the cocoa crop has been illegally sold in neighboring countries such as Togo and Ivory Coast, where prices are higher. Ghana's cocoa output has dropped fifty percent in the last twenty years. To encourage increased production, the government is offering a higher guaranteed price and regular payments to farmers. While the price paid per ton of cocoa on the London market was averaging about $880 between 1966-1970, average Ghanaian producers were receiving only about $280 for their product; less than one-third as much as the sales price.

Zambia and Zaïre have experienced a similar problem with their copper sales on the world market in London. In

Table 4
MINERALS AND AGRICULTURAL PRODUCTS IMPORTED FROM AFRICA TO THE UNITED STATES

Product	% of US Needs Obtained from Africa	Principal Producers	Africa's % of Total World Production
A. *Minerals and Petroleum*			
Columbium	100	Nigeria	
Manganese	99	Gabon, South Africa	14
Cobalt	98	Zaïre	74
Chromium	91	Zimbabwe, South Africa	36
Bauxite (for aluminum	85	Guinea, Ghana, Cameroon	28 (est)
Platinum	80	South Africa	50
Antimony	56	South Africa	49 (est)
Gold	45	Ghana, South Africa	65
Vanadium	36	South Africa	46
Petroleum	35	Nigeria, Algeria, Libya, Angola	10
Diamonds	100	South Africa, Sierra Leone, Ghana, Tanzania, etc.	
Also: copper, iron ore, zinc, tin, lead.			
B. *Agricultural Products*			
Coffee	25	Angola, Ethiopia, Kenya, Uganda, etc.	27
Cocoa	50	Ghana, Nigeria, Cameroon	69
Natural Rubber	Not available	Liberia	5
Sugar	Not available	Swaziland, South Africa, etc.	5
Tea	Not available	Kenya, Tanzania, etc.	16
Cotton	Not available	Sudan	11
Sisal	Not available	Tanzania	52
Tobacco	Not available	Zimbabwe	9
Timber	Not available	Congo, Gabon, Nigeria	5
Pyrethrum	Not available	Kenya, Zimbabwe	100

Sources: World Bank, *Accelerated Development in Sub-Saharan Africa*, Washington, D.C., 1981, and J.S. Whittaker ed. *Africa and the United States*, New York: NYU Press, 1978.

1970 alone, copper fell $750 per ton, necessitating a drastic revision in Zambian plans for spending on development projects and, after 1974, continued into a deep slump.

Every African nation has experienced similar disruptions due to the instability of the world market. Thus, the average agricultural nation is faced with a paradox: the more coffee or peanuts produced, the more likely the price per bag will fall. In the United States this does not happen to most farmers because the government agrees to buy the goods at a guaranteed price in order to save the farmer from bankruptcy. In France and Germany, the governments pay sugar beet farmers about three times the world market price just to preserve the farms. The average United States peanut farmer, too, earns about triple the price per bag paid to African farmers for their crop.

It is not surprising that in the 1970s the African nations have come to a series of global meetings of the Northern hemisphere nations with the poorer Southern hemisphere nations to plead for price guarantees to stabilize the world market for their products. The rich nations refused even to lower the tariffs on goods that they do not produce themselves, such as coffee.

The agricultural nations of Africa are doubly vulnerable, because crops, unlike minerals, are subject to pests, spoilage, and drought. A crop failure means a national income failure. Drought has been a terrible scourge in the 1970s along the edge of the desert, called the Sahel, including Senegal, Mauritania, Mali, Chad, etc., and in the 1980s in East and Southern Africa, from Ethiopia to South Africa. Another problem arises for one-crop economies when the need for that crop is replaced by synthetic products. Mali, Chad, and Tanzania rely on cotton, which has been partially replaced by nylon, dacron, and other synthetic fibers. Tanzania also produces sisal and jute for making rope and sacking. These fibers are being replaced by the plastics. Those nations that depend on the sale of coffee, tea, cloves, peanuts, and oils are

(United Nations photo/Carolyn Redenius)

Single crop economies such as the Cameroon cocoa industry are particularly vulnerable to changes in market prices.

subject to changes of consumers' tastes. Palm oil producers are endangered as detergents replace soaps in the Western supermarket.

THE ROLE OF FOREIGN AID

Direct cash assistance to these poorer nations could help, but all the foreign aid to Africa thus far has been inadequate. One United Nations economist estimated that Africa lost twice as much money because of a fall in prices during the 1950s and 1960s as it gained in aid during that period, and prices paid for African produce and minerals remained low in the 1970s and early 1980s. The amount of aid given by the United States has not been large.

For instance, official United States assistance to developing countries as a percentage of Gross National Product ranked below most other Western industrial nations: It was about one-fifth that of the Netherlands, one-fourth of Norway and Sweden, and less than one-half that of Denmark, France, Belgium, Germany, Britain, Canada, Australia, and Austria. Between 1970 and 1981, the United States development assistance as a percentage of Gross National Product actually declined by more than thirty-five percent.

Table 5

TOTAL UNITED STATES FOREIGN AID GIVEN TO PARTICULAR FOREIGN COUNTRIES AND REGIONS, 1945-1982

Vietnam	$22,873,000,000
Korea	12,555,000,000
France and Germany	11,367,000,000
Sub-Saharan Africa	10,062,000,000

Source: U.S. Agency for International Development, *U.S. Overseas Loans and Grants and Assistance from International Organizations, July 1, 1945 - June 30, 1982*, Washington: U.S. AID, 1982.

Indeed, the total amount of United States assistance to all developing countries was about $4.2 billion in 1977, which was one-seventh the amount spent in the United States that year on alcoholic beverages, one-fourth that spent on tobacco, and less than American expenditures on barbershops, beauty parlors, and bath services. And Africa was not the favored recipient of United States economic assistance. Of the aid given to individual nations in 1979-1980, Israel and Egypt received half of all United States assistance, followed by Turkey, Bangladesh, Indonesia, India, Portugal, Nicaragua, Philippines, and Peru.

Britain and France gave proportionately more aid to their former colonies than did other colonial powers. Yet, African nations prefer to receive an equitable price for the products they produce, rather than to receive aid from the nations that buy those products at low prices.

Africa loses a reasonable return on its goods not only because production and marketing are precarious but also because the middlemen who handle the goods are almost exclusively non-Africans. The banks, shipping companies, warehousing firms, advertisers, and marketers are from the powerful firms of Paris, London, Brussels, and New York; and the profits set aside for themselves are usually significant.

It is generally accepted that wealthier nations should help the poorer nations to develop. As the poorer nations grow economically, they are able to buy the products the wealthier nations are producing: radios, autos, consumer goods, and machinery. The peoples of Africa want more of these goods than their economies can afford. Much of what Africa uses is imported. Nigeria, for instance, produces little wheat, so huge amounts of refined flour must be imported to make the bread Nigerians demand. Ghana is the world's leading producer of cocoa, yet tea is a more popular drink there, and it must be imported. Zaïre and Zambia produce about one-fifth of the world's copper. Until 1970, Zambian copper was exported to Britain, where electrical wire was made and shipped back to Zambia—a twelve thousand mile round trip. Great rejoicing accompanied the 1971 opening of Zambia's new copper wire factory which will supply the needs of East and Central Africa.

President Julius Nyerere of Tanzania summarized this development dilemma:

> Judging by our actions, our national objective seems to be to "catch up with the North," and development seems to mean buying the most elaborate building and the latest invention in every field, regardless of our capacity to pay for it—even to maintain it. Thus we have created a continuing dependency on the importation of technology and spare parts, which then requires us to produce for export regardless of our people's present hunger and present needs. All too frequently an adverse turn in the terms of trade, or a drought, or a simple miscalculation, then causes a major balance of payments crisis. This we try to deal with by urging our people to work harder for the same return, and by borrowing from the North (if we can) in order to invest in the production of greater exports which we hope will pay the old and new debt! Thus we further increase our dependence and our weakness. In the process we create a so-called "modern sector" which we point to as a sign of development. But it exists in a sea of poverty, ignorance and disease. Eventually we are unable to provide even this modern sector with its ever-increasing need for imports from the North, and much less to assuage the demand which its example has created among the surrounding masses. Our economy—modern and traditional sector alike—becomes less and less efficient. Our final position is worse than the first.[4]

ALTERNATE ROUTES TO DEVELOPMENT

Across Africa the demands for better health, housing, and diet are outrunning budgets. The situation in some countries is desperate—caused by rapidly increasing population, higher and higher prices for foreign manufactured goods, and static or decreasing prices for commodities. A series of solutions is being tried across Africa:

1. Diversifying Production of Commodities

The African nations must find alternative crops quickly and begin to mine several minerals instead of one. Primarily, they need to become the processors and manufacturers of products, not just the producers of the raw materials. Since the African peoples are demanding a better life now, most African nations have become increasingly dependent upon the one or two commodities they produce to earn valuable foreign exchange. Profits usually have been used to improve the production of the single commodity rather than to diversify. These nations seek high prices on the world market and yet continue to overproduce, even though they are aware that other countries are also producing more of the same product. This can be seen in the coffee market, where growing production led to a decline in the selling price. Thus far, these nations have not been able to unite to raise the world prices.

2. Decreasing Consumption of Imported Goods

In order to reduce the growing consumption of foreign manufactured goods, many African nations are placing higher taxes on imported goods. Such a policy encourages local businessmen or government agencies to build factories to manufacture their own shirts, shoes, processed foods, cigarettes, beer, pots and pans, cloth, and other basics. In many nations, the government owns all or part of the new factories. Since few individuals in Africa have the technology or the money to invest in such ventures, government financing or participation through government-owned industrial development corporations is necessary. Limiting consumption of foreign goods often is difficult because many people have acquired a taste for Western goods, such as Italian shoes, British cigarettes, Greek canned fish, Swiss watches, English bicycles, Japanese autos and transistor radios, and Hong Kong ball-point pens. The new import duties are added to the already high shipping costs. Thus, a Western life-style costs more in Africa than it does in London or Washington.

Some African nations are beginning to produce hoes, shovels, picks, hand tractors, fertilizer, lanterns, and other articles needed by the poor and the farmers. Still, most nations must import many items used to make these products: paint for lanterns, herbicides and insecticides for commercial farming, tractors and trucks, and steel for shovels and picks. Increasing local production also results in increasing consumption of foreign imported goods.

3. Increased Skills Through Education

The need for education—in science, management, health techniques, agriculture, and teaching itself—consumes much development money. Only a few years ago, over half of every government dollar in western Nigeria was spent on education. Because so many secondary and university teachers must be hired from other nations, the cost of secondary and, especially, university education in Africa is higher per pupil than in any of the wealthier nations. Every African nation, therefore, faces a dilemma—whether to invest in many expensive foreign teachers for a short period in order to train many people at the university and post-secondary technical school level or to invest in education at the primary and junior high school levels using local teachers. Many African nations are putting substantial funds into hiring foreigners to train university students (Nigeria alone has thirteen universities). But there is much disparity in the educational resources of the different nations. The British emphasized education in Nigeria and Ghana. As a result, they have many university graduates. The Belgians and Portuguese, on the other hand, did not create educational systems to meet the development needs of the people in their colonies; therefore, there are few secondary school graduates.

University and secondary graduates pose another problem in Africa because these students aim for a standard of pay equal to that of the former colonial officials with similar education. Many foreigners continue to work in Africa and have helped to set the standard of living which university graduates believe they deserve. This usually includes a comfortable home, a car, and a salary high enough to afford a servant. In Tanzania, President Julius Nyerere attempted to lower consumption levels by ordering all upper level civil servants, including himself, to cut their salaries by ten percent. Still, some economists suggest that the approximately ten percent of the African population which is educated and lives in wealthier African nations consumes about half of the total income in Africa. In the years ahead, it may be difficult to avoid protest, upheaval, and revolution should this imbalance continue. As in other countries, personal favoritism and corruption exist within the political structures of some African countries. The African politicians who engage in such practices will be vulnerable if and when strong opposition develops.

4. Increased Agricultural Production

In order to feed the population adequately, African nations are attempting to achieve greater food production, but a dilemma remains: what is the best way to do this? The three alternatives are: large plantations established by colonial companies; increased support for individual African farmers; or new government-aided cooperatives. The plantation approach probably provides the best immediate return on government investment. Agricultural experts direct each operation and produce large quantities of cash crops, which can be sold abroad. In the 1960s, Africa increased its agricultural production by 2.5 percent per year, and just kept even with population growth. However, agricultural production fell behind population growth in the 1970s and early 1980s.

Providing assistance for the individual farmer is perhaps the best way to increase the diet of the local farmer and the best long-range solution. But this approach requires a complex development program. Because individual farmers are scattered across many miles of territory, it is difficult to provide each with expert agricultural assistance, fertilizers, plowing and harvesting services, and the seed and insecticides that will make farming more productive. These farmers need loans to purchase these necessities. Better roads, telephone and electrical service, and storage and distribution centers are also required.

The third alternative is the producer-cooperative farm on which ten to thirty farm families work together in the same fields on the same crops under expert financial and technological support from the government. Such centralized cooperatives make it easier to provide needed services, while allowing the people to feel a sense of pride in owning their own farm. In order to make the farmer's life more secure, many governments now are guaranteeing a fixed price for a farmer's crops so that the fluctuating world market will not create similar fluctuations in the cooperatives' income. In the cooperative, one well-trained member can easily train others. Specialization also occurs when various members of the cooperative supervise particular activities or tasks, such as seeding, fertilizing, using mechanical equipment, insect control, marketing, and bookkeeping. Still, the process of establishing the cooperatives is a difficult one. The farmers are not immigrants, as are those people who enter the similar Israeli kibbutz cooperative farms. The African farmers bring with them their attachment to a special area, to their kin living in the same township, perhaps to burial grounds nearby, and to older techniques of bush-fallowing and slash-and-burn agriculture handed down from generation to generation. Among some African peoples there are traditions of individual farming and landholding. Nevertheless, when these new cooperatives and village relocation schemes do provide better standards of living, they will become more popular. But the process of change is slow. In Tanzania, a country most committed to cooperative development, more than five percent of the total population has been brought into the *ujamaa* plan of cooperatives. This is a start, but a better life will come slowly. During the 1960s when many farmers moved to cooperatives with high hopes of increased standards of living, Tanzania was losing $75 million on the world market through the drop in prices for cotton, coffee, and sisall. The war in Uganda to unseat dictator Idi Amin Dada set Tanzania even farther behind economically.

The road ahead for agricultural development is long and arduous. Production remains at a very low level. Africa's land area is over three times that of the United States, but it has only three percent of the agricultural productivity of the United States. In 1983 Zimbabwe was the only nation in Africa able to feed itself without importing food. All of the various efforts for development of agriculture in the 1980s will be valuable if they result in a diet that has an egg a week, more meat, and a growing variety of nutritious foods.

CONCLUSION

A number of dilemmas continue to face the African economist. Each year African governments must decide where to invest their scarce resources—in social welfare, cash-crop schemes, economic infrastructure, peasant agriculture, or in industrialization. The people demand more and better hospitals, more water systems, old age pensions, injury and disability insurance, infant health plans, sewerage systems, and telephone service. Yet, these improvements do not earn dollars on the world market. In order to earn money, some nations emphasize the cash-crop or mineral schemes, frequently requesting services from foreign companies. This method earns cash, but it does not advance the training, managerial skills, and general welfare of the local population. Other nations emphasize economic infrastructure—the building of the basic ports, warehouses, roads, repair shops for trucks, railroads, and communications systems, which do not earn money in and of themselves, but which are necessities for developing large economies. These investments, however, have no immediate return in terms of a better life for the African people. The peoples' demands for a better life *now* make such choices difficult. The economists may emphasize peasant development programs aimed at people and not the structures of industrial development. Again, cash is not produced by such programs, but some individual welfare is. To these, the development planner must add funds to industrialize, to build new factories for the manufacture of consumer goods, and to purchase agricultural equipment. The lack of funds for such projects frequently means that the African governments request foreign companies to build, operate, and profit from the plants.

African governments vary in their emphasis on these various development patterns. No one plan and no unique development scheme contain the magic answer to achieve satisfaction and happiness today or tomorrow. Africa is developing, and a better standard of living is being created. There are less diseases, a longer life span, lower infant mortality, better diets, and better housing than existed twenty years ago. But the great leaps forward occur only in the few rich nations. In comparison, most African nations are standing still. As long ago as 1967, the Foreign Minister of Ivory Coast said, "These young countries realize that whatever their efforts, and whatever aid they may receive, the gap which separates them from rich countries is widening relentlessly."

4

AFRICAN SOCIETIES: MYTHS AND REALITIES

An old man is one who remembers when people were more important than machines.
Zimbabwean Proverb

By the time the colonial powers arrived, African societies already were undergoing rapid social change. The newcomers brought more change through the slave trade; through the gun and dynamite, which upset the balance of powers; through forced labor, taxation, and migration; and through the schools. The result has been a dynamic change sweeping across the continent. New cities, industries, and markets have emerged. However, many people outside Africa have difficulty seeing beyond the common myths and images of African societies and recognizing the new realities.

MYTHS OF SAVAGE AFRICA

Throughout the popular media, African people are sometimes depicted as strange people, who look different from "normal" people, eat strange foods, and never developed materially.

Many movies, travel books, and textbooks feature pictures of people who are different. Just like the tourist who wants to photograph the scenes and sites that are different from those at home, the media and textbooks about Africa often focus on the people who are different—especially the so-called "pygmies" and "bushmen."

Many of the "pygmies" of Zaïre are Mbuti peoples, and they do not always stay in the forests as many books would suggest. They frequently work as truck drivers, as traders, and as soldiers in the Zaïrean Army, in which they belong to an elite battalion. The so-called "bushmen" of the Kalahari Desert in South Africa, Botswana, and Namibia are respected for their marvelous adaptation to living in the harsh conditions of the desert. They are Khoi-Khoi and San people. Some still live in the desert, but many work as farm laborers and mine workers. Their adaptation to the desert was forced on them over a century ago when they were chased off their pastures and farm land by the white farmers and migrating African people in southern Africa.

African diets are different from our own, but usually not in ways we expect. Today, about eighty percent of the average African diet is starch—grains like wheat and corn or potato-like roots and tubers. Across the African continent, the major diet deficiency is protein. Africa is not endowed with large numbers of natural harbors, undulating coastlines, or natural lakes—all of which provide good fishing grounds. In many areas, the tsetse fly kills or infects cattle and game. As a result, in times of food shortage, some Africans have sought to supplement their diet with oil and protein-rich locusts, caterpillars, flying ants, and small mammals which Westerners do not normally eat. As with culture and civilization, a "strange" diet exists only in the eyes of the beholder. Many African people are mystified and sickened by the willingness of Westerners to eat frog, crab, lobster, and even snakemeat. As one Zambian commented, "How can people who eat those things be civilized?"

Many Americans and Europeans believe that Africa is a continent of inferior peoples because it never developed the railroads, highways, electronics, automobiles, and material comforts of Western countries. It is true that the *material* accomplishments are unequal. Many factors prevented some African societies from focusing energy and resources on material invention and production: infertile land, which made life very insecure; tropical diseases uncommon in the colder Northern hemisphere; lack of large-scale agricultural surpluses; and, most important, the emphasis in many African societies on equality, sharing of resources, and building relatively classless societies.

In spite of these factors, Africa did experience many great material accomplishments, especially in construction and building processes which were admirably adapted to the African terrain: the huge towering stone temples and enclosures in Zimbabwe, constructed without use of mortar; the majestic Islamic mosques in West Africa; and the beautiful cast bronze sculptures of Ife and Benin in Nigeria. There have also been many health and medical treatments from natural sources. But rather than attempting to compare European material accomplishments with those of Africa, we need to understand African values beyond materialism.

The most important fact about African civilization is its emphasis on individuals, their value and their equality. African societies developed most fully in concepts of justice; in the practice of giving all persons their due; in establishing solidarity and community in the village; in satisfying the most basic human needs for fellowship and comraderie; and in understanding the incredibly complex human social linkages.

To deal with the thief and the criminal, for example, African societies developed complex legal systems with one goal in mind—to restore those on trial to their rightful places in society. A criminal act frequently meant that the whole village was on trial for letting malice and greed creep into the village through the actions of the guilty party. At the end of many trials, the accused and the aggrieved party must agree with the verdict, and the two must then embrace or shake hands and exchange gifts as symbols of the restoration of each to his original place of trust and brotherhood.

The great complexity of African lineage systems still amazes Western anthropologists. Just when the ethnographers believe they have mastered the highly sophisticated African ways of tracing social bonds with a neighboring village, a new complexity is discovered. But throughout the lineage system, the underlying principle remains apparent—the need to find a means of understanding that "we all are of a common cloth." The result of such interrelatedness is that people better understand their ties, their common sources, and their interdependence with one another. Even in African societies where slavery did exist, it was generally less oppressive than American slavery. In Africa, the slave usually was accorded legal rights, and his children were not necessarily enslaved. Civilization in Africa thus developed in terms of complex inter-societal human relationships.

THE NEW CITIES AND TOWNS OF AFRICA

Although three-fourths of Africa's population is rural, the cities are growing rapidly.

After independence in 1960 to 1980, the sub-Saharan nations found their urban population almost doubling from eleven to twenty-one percent. By 1980 a major portion of the population of several nations lived in urban areas: over forty percent of the Congo and Central African Republic; over a third of the population of Zaïre, Ghana, Liberia, Zambia, Cameroon, and the Ivory Coast; and over one-fifth of Africa's most populous nation, Nigeria. These new urbanites came seeking jobs, schools, and better health care. This does not mean that life is universally better in town. Conditions are very bad in the expanding shantytowns or squatter settlements found near most African cities. As in the United States, urban African housing is segregated according to income. Wealthy suburbs have large green lawns with comfortable two-story or ranch-type homes, gardens, fruit

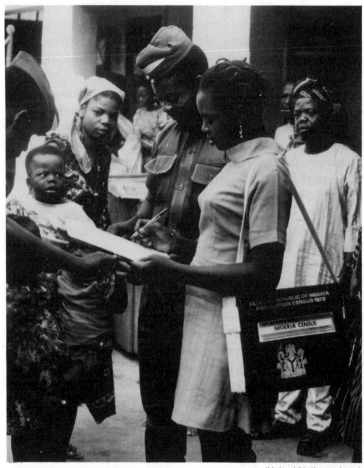

(United Nations photo)

The shifting structure of the population in many nations requires govern-mental efforts to collect demographic information.

trees, and well-lighted, paved streets. In many parts of Africa, these suburbs were the white areas before independence. Now, wealthy African businessmen, government officials, university professors, and others have joined the remaining Europeans.

One step down the income scale are the apartments and small bungalows of the new urban middle class. These include those who have a secondary education as well as many administrators, foremen, typists, clerks, supervisors, salesmen, and party officials. In an attempt to meet the needs of these new groups, African governments and individual investors have built new housing. These areas may have electricity and running water, but the streets may not be paved. Nor do these small concrete-block or stucco houses have the room, comfort, or style found in the elite housing.

Another step down the income scale is mass housing, huge areas of three-room houses each with an outdoor water spigot and privy. Here live the taxi drivers, small hawkers, clergy, primary school teachers, junior clerks, and common laborers of the new towns. These houses almost always are overcrowded with large families and kin who have not found housing elsewhere. Because of the acute housing shortage in the towns, anyone who has such a house is considered fortunate. But conditions are not good here. These are the houses that the colonial and private company builders thought were adequate for African needs. The house was part of the job. If a man lost his job, he and the family also lost the house. This, of course, made him cautious about offending the employer. Today these complexes frequently have no sewerage service, unpaved streets, and few social amenities. There is little grass or vegetation, only mud and dust. Keeping clean is very difficult.

Many people at this occupational level live in the surrounding shantytowns. These houses are illegally built on any available land. They are constructed from canvas and cardboard, pieces of corrugated tin, or concrete block, and, more commonly, of Kimberly-brick (dried clay blocks, mortared together with mud). In such townships or squatter areas, sanitary conditions are terrible. Outdoor toilets are used, and impure water is drawn from shallow wells. As quickly as these shanty houses are vacated by persons who are fortunate enough to be given one of the new, small, government-constructed bungalows, it is reoccupied by newly arrived villagers who have come in hopes of finding work in town.

Transportation is stratified, too. At the top, the government ministers and executives may ride in a chauffeured Mercedes. The junior ministers and high civil servants ride in the government Peugeots and larger British cars. The lesser civil servants have Volkswagens, British Miniminors, Italian Fiats, or small French Renaults. The masses of people walk, ride bicycles, and use the less dependable and inadequate bus systems. Most African towns badly need new mass transportation systems.

It is this stratification of privilege that bedevils every African nation and leads many to plead for a turn to the political ideology of African socialism. African socialism is appealing because it offers a policy of equality, especially in lands where the contrast between the elites and the poor is extreme. It calls for elimination of special privileges for private investors and the educated. It also promises to everyone the basic needs of food, health care, and shelter. It is in the face of this inequality and this hunger for the "good" life that the new African societies are being formed. The socialist ideologies have a strong appeal because of their promise to narrow the gap between rich and poor.

TRADITIONAL AFRICAN SOCIAL LIFE

For over a century, we have read that all "Africans live in tribes." Unfortunately, the term is a bad word to describe African societies. Even worse, it carries the connotation of uncivilized, dangerous, uncontrolled, superstitious human beings unlike ourselves. Yet most of the African visitors we meet in the United States or in Africa seem to behave much like we do. They speak English, drive cars, worship in churches, send their children to school, dress in business suits, and interact easily in American society. What is the truth of the nature of African societies? Are these business-suited, articulate African visitors only "tribesmen in camou-flage"?

The word "tribe" has been used by scholars from the West to describe peoples living in smaller societies with less material technology than our own. Thus, "tribes" are found in North America, Southeast Asia, ancient Israel, the hills and deserts of the Middle East, and, most of all, in Africa. However, we can find no definition in the scholarly literature of anthropology that really describes these societies. Some say that tribespeople have a common ancestor; others believe tribes have a common language; some say persons who live under a chieftain are tribal; and others say tribes share a common government or common culture. In fact, when we look at the societies of Africa, we find none of the these definitions fits all of the societies that existed before colonial rule. Most do not trace themselves to a common ancestor. Many societies include peoples with different languages and dialects, and many people in different rural societies in fact speak the same dialect. Many of these societies do not have chiefs or have only chieftaincies conveniently created by the colonial government. Some of Africa's "tribes" consist of millions of people, while others consist of less than one hundred people. For these reasons, scholars prefer to discard the term "tribe" because it is misleading and creates an image of an inferior and sub-human people. In fact, Africa's small-scale societies are much like the clans of Scotland or the villages of Ireland and Wales, whose people are not called "tribal." More appropri-ate terms are societies, ethnicities, classes, or simply the name of the people such as the Yoruba or the Lunda.

Most African societies consider themselves not so much members of a society as of a *nation* and a lineage—persons who trace their kinship through their father, mother, grandparents, great grandparents, etc. However, many other African people consider uncles, aunts, cousins, great aunts and uncles, and second cousins, etc. to be more important members of the "extended family." Members of the extended family help each other with payments of taxes and school fees; costs of celebrations of marriages, births, and deaths; finding jobs; planting and harvest labor; and many other tasks.

Some bilateral groups such as the Lozi of Zambia trace their lineage to their ancestors just as Americans do—through the line of their mothers and fathers, valuing each equally. Other societies are matrilineal, tracing their heritage through the mother's side of the family. Others are patrilineal, tracing through the father's side. In matrilineal societies, for instance, a young boy needing school fees or a bus fare home may rightfully approach his mother's brother instead of his father for money. The father will be responsible for helping his sisters' children. While these are the formal rules of matrilineal societies, many urban matrilineal peoples actually turn to one's own father for help, just as in Western countries. Other customs differ among the different ethnic groups.

Loyalty in such societies is first to one's kin, defined as all those uncles and aunts, cousins and second-cousins, and distantly related "brothers." These systems provided food and care for everyone—sick and crippled, young and aged, good farmers and bad—through their kinship ties to one another. This was important in an insecure environment with widespread tropical disease and (for much of the continent) uncertain growing conditions and frequent drought. As new forms of society have developed in the new nations of Africa, these laws and customs have changed. But even in their changed forms, they remain absolutely essential to village

(United Nations photo)

Some aspects of social interaction still take place at the village and kinship level.

society. For instance, when the men are away at the mines or plantations, the kinship members step in to help the father-less family in times of need. In return, the migrant laborer sends a portion of his paycheck back to the village to support his family and to help with the other members of his lineage who remain there. The absent laborer helps with the school fees of his nephew, whose mother shares her garden produce with the lonely family of the laborer.

Increasingly, however, in independent Africa (though not in white-dominated nations) labor is less migratory because the new governments encourage families to live together in the town where the laborer works. The colonial pattern of bachelor barracks was not a happy situation. But even when the family lives together in town, the rural kinship system is not destroyed. It takes on new functions.

Throughout the twentieth century, African urban life has been unstable. Not only were disease, diet, and housing conditions worse in town, but urban life was terribly insecure. If an African urbanite was injured, there was no disability insurance to support him. Unemployment was not cushioned by compensation. Unions were either outlawed or under-mined by the increasing stream of rural immigrants who were happy to take the place of striking union members. No social security was available to make old age more secure. And because the town was so full of strangers from different districts and foreign nations, there seemed to be no one to assist the needy in times of sickness, injury, financial need, or death in the family. This great insecurity was made worse by the poverty and poor working conditions of colonial Africa. Alternate sources of security—lineage groups, religious organizations, political parties, and other associations were formed in response.

The kinship ties to the village were strengthened because many men planned to return to their villages in their retirement years, remembering them as the place of ease, enjoyment, and friendship with other kinsmen and neighbors.

Others sent gifts back home and visited only occasionally in
order to insure for their old age the right to some land, a
house, and possibly some cattle. The ties to the village were
maintained as social insurance against disaster, loss of job,
or injury to the family's breadwinner.

ETHNICITY IN TOWN

Since loyalty was primarily to one's kin or village,
ethnicity emerged primarily in town, where a man encountered
crowds of people with different languages, customs, and
beliefs. To deal with other groups, social categories or labels
were used. These labels usually denoted a man's home area
or language and became his ethnic group. Furthermore, in
town, the European employer asked, "What is your tribe?"
In some instances, one's tribe actually was created by the
administration. In the former Belgian Congo (now Zaïre),
there was a group of river villages which were referred to by
the local people as "Banglala." Belgian officials recruited
men for work on the river in transport and construction.
These men were referred to as "Banglala" and had the
reputation of being good workers. This image of Banglala as
"good workers" spread among the African men seeking
work, and many called themselves "Banglala" in order to
strengthen their chances of being hired. The Banglala "tribe"
was born out of peculiar circumstances having nothing to do
with kinship.

Thus, the men were labeled with a tribe name even if it was
not meaningful to them. They also formed "ethnic associations," sometimes at the encouragement of the colonial
officials, who thought these ties would minimize the disruption of town life. In some nations these associations became a
link with home. At association meetings, a man could find
others who spoke the same language. Frequently, the
association served as a savings club. Also a man could learn
of job possibilities and news from the home district. Most of

all, the association was a base for mutual care, concern, and respect in the cold impersonal world of the cosmopolitan city. Thus, ethnicity had developed, whereby men became proud of their home area and identified with other men who had similar language, home areas, and customs, even if they had not done so at home in the village.

This ethnicity is well-known in American cities. Immigrants who came from provinces in Italy as far apart as Tuscany and Sicily suddenly belonged together as "Italian-Americans," living in the same neighborhood, belonging to a nationality club together, voting for a candidate who promised to help "Italian-Americans," telling each other of jobs, and celebrating together. Similarly, Afro-Americans, Irish-Americans, Mexican-Americans, Chinese-Americans, and all the other immigrant groups are important in the politics and economy of the American city for uniting persons of diverse villages, states, provinces, and nations. These new identities have little or no meaning in the "old country," but they are very important for survival in the city in the competitive search for jobs, political power, housing, and schools. Ethnic identity in African cities, towns, and nations is very similar.

URBANIZATION AND ETHNICITY

As identification with an ethnic group in town takes on new meaning and importance, the hold of the village and, sometimes, of kinship is lessened. The particular customs, laws, and political leaders of the home village sometimes become much less important. In 1967, an article appeared in the *Times of Zambia:*

> A Zambian senior chief, who is visiting the Copperbelt, is depressed by the welcome Copperbelt people give their chiefs. "Most of the enthusiasm has now gone," he said in Ndola yesterday, before he left for Chingola. . . . He said few people now came to meet the

chief. . . . "It's not like the old days," he said. . . . The
46-year-old chief visits the Copperbelt at least every
three years. On his recent tour, he met only 500
people.[5]

In town, new courts and judges made most of the chiefs'
courts unnecessary. The new national political parties also
replaced the rural politics and officials. Throughout the
town, too, men were learning to speak other African languages such as Swahili or Lingala, English, or French in
order to participate in the trade unions and the politics, to
greet neighbors, and to worship together in churches and
mosques. When rural officials came to town to interfere in
union and party affairs, they frequently were asked to leave
or, in some instances, were actually chased away from an
area in which they "had no business." New languages also
meant intertribal contact of boys with girls. As a result in
many African towns a high proportion of marriages now
were between persons from different villages who spoke
different languages. The children of these marriages then had
a choice: they could identify with the ethnic group of their
mother or their father or, more likely, not really identify with
either. (Of course when asked by the colonial official, they
still could say, "I'm a Yoruba, sir." But the meaning was
gone.) The loss of dances, songs, customs, stories, and other
culture of the village has been so extensive that some
governments have founded national departments of culture
and art to encourage appreciation for the old ways and
customs. These government agencies seek to capture with
tape recorders and films the history and lore in oral traditions
and customs before those who remember them die, and the
traditions are lost.

In the place of these rural ways are the cosmopolitan tastes
of the city, the nation, and a mixture of Western, Middle
Eastern, and African customs. In Nigerian towns we may
see European fashions, levis, Arab style robes, and the
agbada (a traditional Nigerian dress). The music may be an

American soul-singer or the popular "high life," (a shuffle dance to two-beat music). Yet, the ethnicity persists. Why?

THE IMPORTANCE OF ETHNICITY

Ethnicity in the urban area remains strong because it is a means of identifying people, of categorizing strangers, of obtaining favors, and of acquiring help in times of insecurity. Just as the Irishman enjoys the "wearing of the green" on St. Patrick's Day, and a Scotsman wears traditional plaids, peoples of Africa are proud of their home areas and the dances, songs and reputations of the people. When a group from the home area forms a new soccer team to compete in city tournaments, they cheer for "our boys" in the same way that fans of the New York Mets, Dallas Cowboys, Los Angeles Lakers, or even a high school cheer for "our team."

People without jobs also can use ethnicity to gain employment. If normal applications for work fail, it is natural to turn to a family tie—to an uncle or aunt or to another relative who is in a position to help find or to offer a job. The colonial governments of Africa employed particular language or ethnic groups in the police, army, railroad, or as clerks in the government. They thereby established the dominance of one group in a particular place or type of occupation. When jobs become scarce, as is the case all over Africa today, people from the same home area learn about new openings first and may be given preference over other competitors from a different ethnic or language group.

Finally, ethnicity develops in the political process. Politicians of all nations will use almost any appeal to win votes, especially when the elected post has a good salary. Some politicians in Africa will appeal either overtly or covertly for support from the same ethnic group. When such a man has been elected with ethnic support, he is expected to serve those interests and to hand out political jobs to those who supported him. As a result, many elections in Africa are clouded with cries of "tribalism," "nepotism," and "corruption"—by which the accusers mean that another group is trying to gain a competitive advantage for itself in the fight for scarce jobs. To undercut such charges, many African leaders choose one member from each minority group for the political cabinet. Thus, what we choose to call "tribalism" in Africa is much like "ethnicity" in Europe, "minority groups" in New York, and "regionalism" throughout America.

MAGIC AND RITUAL IN AFRICAN LIFE

Belief in magic is not unique to Africa. In Western nations, many believe that the location of stars and planets, as catalogued in horoscopes, can foretell the future; that tea leaves in a cup or interpretations of tarot cards can reveal the future; or that a rabbit's foot or lucky charm can provide protection from bad fortune.

Part of the mystique of African societies is their supposed reliance on magic. So pervasive is this stereotype that the word "voodoo" (a term rightly applied to a practice of magic in Haiti in the Caribbean) is often used to create images of "black magic" in Africa. Actually, African societies are not so radically different from others in this regard. Most societies hold some form of belief in magic. Just as Africans appeal to spirits of ancestors for guidance and a good harvest, Americans, too, pray for the health and safety of a close relative who is in danger. Magic and ritual are very much a part of both American and African life as a means of dealing with danger, death, and other fears.

Magic and ritual are common in Africa because life can be so vulnerable and uncertain. With the world's highest birth and death rates, it is not surprising that some Africans invoke the supernatural to relieve anxiety. The local herbalist, who has been incorrectly called a witchdoctor, has a potion, an amulet, or perhaps a magical stone to allay a patient's fear of the future or to make that uncertainty more endurable. This small relief from fear and uncertainty may be enough to help the individual take control of his world and his life with courage and calm.

RELIGIOUS ORGANIZATIONS

Religion in the African village is a ritual of life. Passage from one phase of life to another is marked by ceremonial rituals—at birth, initiation and circumcision, marriage, and death. Ceremonies are also held at the time of planting and harvest. In the rituals, the villagers celebrate their ties to kinsmen, ancestors, and the universe. It is one more way of binding people to one another and to the duties and tasks that will serve the needs of the whole community. Thus, one's duties as husband, wife, worker, ruler, and worshipper are defined and given importance in the rituals of village life. In many African religions, the emphasis is on accepting the goodness of one's society and its rulers, to performing one's duties without complaint, and, above all, to resisting the temptation to harbor evil thoughts that would disrupt the village.

The way in which African societies deal with the presence of evil is an important religious function. Other African beliefs aim to protect or restore health. A number of types of traditional healers use special roots and herbs as medicines. Some of these have natural medical value. They mix special formulas in much the same way as the nineteenth-century American patent medicine men mixed their secret formula elixirs. Their medicines are intended to make their patient more attractive to the opposite sex, to restore fertility, to protect babies from colds, to relieve headaches, fever and other ailments, and to safeguard the traveler. Many of their medical practices are being studied to understand their chemical and psychological efficacy.

The image of the white missionary working in a remote village (Dr. Albert Schweitzer inoculating African children in the thick jungle), mirrors the familiar idea of the white man "bearing his burden." Missionaries now are seen by many Africans as those who came with the colonialists to eradicate African religion in the same way the companies crippled African agriculture and the colonial governments remade village social and political life. In the white settled areas of southern Africa, Africans lament: "When you first came, you had the Bible and we had the land. Now we have the Bible and you have the land." There is no doubt that missionaries were used by some colonizers. Cecil Rhodes is reported to have suggested that missionaries were better than policemen—and cheaper! Traders, settlers, and missionaries brought religious faiths that have taken root on the African continent—Christianity in Central, West, and southern Africa and Islam in North, West, and East Africa. It also is true that the land and riches were claimed by the miners and settlers, whose white missionary compatriots preached acceptance of "civilization" and rejection of the pagan past. There are instances of missionaries speaking in behalf of Africans, protecting them from certain colonial or company actions, but missionaries were generally sympathetic to the colonial policies and goals.

The general pattern of religion in Africa is clear today. The broad sweep of North African Islam extends south into Senegal, Mali, Upper Volta, Niger, Nigeria, Chad, Sudan, Uganda, Kenya, and Somalia, and down the east coast in Tanzania, Malawi, and Mozambique. Below that group of countries and in their southern portions are found traditional faiths—believers in the ancestors and spirit-worship—and Christians. In Africa as a whole, Muslims are one and a half times as numerous as Christians. However, most Africans are not registered in any religious organizations. In Africa south of the Sahara Desert, however, there are more Christians than Muslims, and more Catholics than Protestants.

Islam expanded across the Sahara into West Africa through Muslim traders and missionaries from the Islamic schools of North Africa. Christianity gradually was replaced in North Africa and parts of West and East Africa by Islam, except among the Egyptian Copts and the Christian kingdom of Ethiopia. Like Christianity, Islam is a universal religion not bound by the language, beliefs, or history of one particular people. Islam taught Arabic as a universal language, which could be used along the trade routes. In the colonial period, the identification of Christianity with the colonial powers created a natural appeal for Islam. Islam could claim to be a religion of the dark-skinned peoples of the world. More importantly, it did not require the convert to break sharply with African traditions and customs. Christian mission schools, on the other hand, brought a pietist moralism to their converts, teaching Western morality as well as Christian belief. The local Christian pastor checked his converts to see that they remained monogamous, did not pay "marriage prices," abstained from alcoholic beverages and tobacco, and did not participate in village dancing and initiation ceremonies. The Koranic schools of Islam did not teach literacy in European languages or arithmetic and the other skills needed for governing the new nations. Gradually those with Christian mission training became the teachers, clerks, administrators, and other officials at the head of sub-Saharan African states. Christians were found in administrative positions even in countries with strong Muslim populations such as Tanzania and Chad.

Even though the forms of Christian belief and practice were alien and very Western in form, Christianity did take root in sub-Saharan Africa. As the religion of the school, it has provided the means to the good life. To go to school was also to attend chapel, to read the Bible, and to pray regularly. There is still a Christian flavor to national celebrations and ceremonies in some countries.

The missionary control of the African churches, however, was a burden and a stigma on the church that retarded Africanization of the ritual, belief, and practice. White control of the churches resulted in a number of schisms from the missions in the early twentieth century. These African Independent Churches protested a number of issues: the insistence on Western morality by prohibiting both polygamy and the drinking of African beer; the refusal of whites to give Africans power in the church; racial discrimination in schools; church taxes; and the cultural sterility in Africa of American, French, or British Christianity. One after another, hundreds of Christian pastors, deacons, and laymen broke away to found new churches. Some of these retained the same ritual, offices, and church order as the missions from which they separated, except they had black leaders. These churches included the Blackman's Presbyterian Church, the African Episcopal Church, and the African Catholic Martyrs Church. The churches grew rapidly in the towns among the educated people in the colonial period, especially in South Africa and Zimbabwe. Because the poor in the towns and in the changing rural areas were satisfied neither with their own village libations to the spirits nor with the formalistic worship of the missions, other new African churches were formed. In these churches, men and women could sing, pray, and "feel the work of the spirit." They could shout for joy, sing praises, use cymbals, dance, and have hands laid on them by the elders to heal the wounded spirit or body and cast out the troubling demons. These new churches developed wherever rapid social change had thrown the older religious and social organizations of the village into chaos. In these truly African churches, those who missed the old ways and who had little chance of material success in urban wage labor found a place to feel at home. They found a new community of persons of different villages who shared a common belief and ritual and who could help one another in times of sickness and need in the new towns. Those churches are growing rapidly in South Africa, Nigeria, Ghana, Kenya, Zambia, and Zimbabwe, wherever the pace of social change has accelerated and Western impact has been extensive.

Probably more than four thousand such Christian movements and churches have been founded in Africa in the past
twenty years.

Christianity's influence on Africa is so great that the rapid
growth of the African churches, both those established by the
missions and those formed independently, may make sub-
Saharan Africa the most Christian continent in the world by
the year 2000.

5

EDUCATION IN AFRICA

They [the whites] ... were strange people ... they destroyed and they constructed. On the black continent it began to be understood that their true power lay not in the cannons of the first morning but rather in what followed the cannons ... the new school ... Better than the cannon, it makes conquest permanent. The cannon compels the body, the school bewitches the soul.[6]

The sailing ship brought white people to Africa. The pistol, rifle, and gunboat made their immediate triumph possible. But it was, unexpectedly, the school that made the conquest permanent. Now that independence has come to almost all of Africa, the school is crucial to the development of the nation. The African teacher today is seeking a truly African education, which will be relevant both to African culture and to the critical need for science and technology. That struggle for meaningful education is primarily a struggle to transform the colonial educational system.

THE COLONIAL SCHOOL

The reactions of the African people to the school have been varied. On the basis of these reactions we may isolate three different stages of educational development: the period of resistance, the period of elite formation, and the period of widespread demand for universal education.

The period of resistance began with the first Portuguese contacts with Africa. The colonial school was not a neutral

78

institution, and it was seen as a part of the colonial system. The missionaries established the school as an instrument of Christianity. In the schools, the African converts were to learn the scriptures, just as the converts to Islam in East, West, and North Africa for centuries had memorized Koranic verses. Thus, the early missionaries brought Western moral training and rote memorization of scriptures along with the enlightenment of literacy. Many early missionaries also taught geography, some rudimentary history of Europe or the world, and arithmetic.

In this period, officials of the colonial governments and of the large mining and plantation corporations had differing goals from those of the missionaries. For these officials, education was a tool by which Africans could become useful manpower. Most African labor was utilized for sheer muscle-power—pulling boats, carrying merchandise, digging trenches, cutting roads, and other manual labor needed for the colonial and company development. Since there were too few Europeans to do all of the clerical work, Africans were employed in offices as well. Later, Africans were used for the simple bookkeeping tasks of the colonial ministries, the railways, the mines, and plantations. The schools were expected to teach these needed skills. The early colonials also wanted the school to teach that colonial rule and company profit-making were legitimate, benevolent, and in the best interests of the African peoples.

African villagers frequently saw the school for what it was—a means for European missionaries, colonials, and profit-makers to achieve their own goals. This is not to suggest that Europeans agreed among themselves about how Africans should be treated. Missionaries, corporations, and colonial governments argued among themselves about the uses and abuses of African workers. Frequently, the missionaries were closer to rural African life, and they championed African interests. However, many missionaries also felt that Westernization, industry, and colonial order were in

(United Nations photo)

Schools were often used by colonial governments in an effort to create a pool of skilled workers. Missionaries created schools of their own to advance Christianity.

the best interest of Africans, and they made decisions on this premise without consulting the Africans.

It is not surprising that there was early African resistance to wage labor and to the school. The labors were arduous; the wages were pitifully low—too low to purchase expensive imported tools and cloth. Wage labor and schooling necessitated leaving one's village and kinsmen, as well as the security that went with them. Some African parents saw the school as a place of bad moral standards, especially in the societies that did not believe in mixing girls and boys until puberty. Furthermore, Africans had their own schools before colonialism. Koranic schools taught the young to memorize the sacred book of Islam, the Koran, and promoting basic literacy in Arabic. Many African peoples had their own designated village teachers to instruct children in the ways of being a mature adult. For boys this meant learning to hunt, to care for cattle, to fish, and to rotate crops, as well as some basic sex education. For girls, it meant learning childcare and homecrafts—cooking, cleaning, home-building—and some basic sex education. For both boys and girls, education in the village included learning the history of their people—the traditions, songs, dances, symbols, and myths, which together constituted the philosophy or religion of that people. It was here that the African way of life was communicated. Thus, resistance to the school often developed because boys and girls would not learn the essentials of African village schooling. Different religious and human values were taught in the European schools. This was a threat to the authority of the village elders and to the tightly-knit fabric of village social life. There, however, important exceptions to the pattern of resistance. For instance, when the Manikongo king was converted to Catholicism by Portuguese Jesuits, he requested full access to European ways—schools, cathedrals, clothing, and some change of custom. In spite of this openness to new ways, these people at the mouth of the Congo River later were virtually annihilated when they stood in the way of Portuguese slave-trading expeditions.

During the period of elite formation, the first groups of educated Africans were trained, many of whom became important leaders in their countries. In Liberia, Sierra Leone, Ghana, and Nigeria, this occurred around 1850, while in the settler and mining territories of East and Central Africa, it occurred during the 1930s and 1940s. The periods varied because of the different policies of the colonial and settler governments.

The French had assimilated Africans into the French system as guaranteed by the French Constitution: ". . . all men, without distinction of color, domiciled in French colonies, are French citizens, and enjoy all the rights assured by the constitutions." The ideal of equality, however, did not ensure equal education for all. The West African French colonies did not institute mass education as in France. In fact, separate plans developed for each colony. The Ivory Coast was to become an agricultural enclave with education appropriate to farm employment. Benin and Senegal were to be the source of an urban administrative elite, especially for Dakar, the "African capital of France." The earliest African education was for the children of chiefs and other elites. But others clamored for the right to schooling, especially those Africans returning from Brazil. These two groups, the children of the rulers and the returned slaves, as well as other urban Africans who happened to live near the very few secondary schools, gradually formed the new educated elite. Eventually they inherited positions of leadership in the government.

The French system differs from the educational systems of the British, Portuguese, and Belgians. First, the French were committed to creating a "complete Frenchman" in their African schools; therefore, while they did not create as many primary schools as were created in the British areas, there was relatively more development of secondary education.

Some Africans went to France for their university education. Some writers suggest that the educated elite of French areas are "Black Frenchmen." It is true that the level of French language ability was quite excellent there. French was the language of instruction from the first year of primary school. In British and Belgian areas, a more varied language policy developed. Some children were taught by missionaries using the local African language for the first four grades of primary school, which meant the students had less acquaintance and facility with the European languages. The French were anxious to avoid creating a class of urban unemployed Africans with low levels of education: thus, there were fewer primary schools in French areas. In the British colonies, the rapid growth of primary education required much greater reliance on African teachers, many of whom had only a few more years of primary education than their students. In such primary classes, very little English was used. The result of the French system was the creation of a small, French-speaking African elite with secondary and university education. The masses remained uneducated and illiterate. The cities of the former French colonies illustrate the effects of that educational system. There are elite sections where educated Africans and Frenchmen live together, but there is very little middle-class housing between the elite section and the poorest urban slums, where the uneducated live.

The Belgians also closely controlled their educational systems. The large Brussels-based corporations that operated the giant mining, plantation, and farm industries in the Congo (now Zaïre) needed, on the one hand, secretaries, file clerks, and supervisors with an academic education, and, on the other hand, mechanics, carpenters, bricklayers, and other artisans with technical education. The Congolese educational system reflected these needs. Over half of the school-age population was in primary school just before independence in 1960. But very little secondary education developed except for practical trades and crafts. University

education was virtually non-existent. When independence
was established in 1960, tropical Africa's largest nation had
no African doctors or army sergeants, and fewer than fifty
persons with a university degree of any kind.

The British colonies had the least regulation and the
greatest variation in educational levels. Many Africans who
were freed from slave ships and set ashore lived in Freetown,
Sierra Leone; in Accra on the Gold Coast (Ghana); and in
Lagos, Nigeria. Some slaves who had been educated in the
United States, Britain, and the West Indies returned to
Africa and assumed positions in the colonial governments.
Because many whites died of malaria or yellow fever soon
after their arrival, much of the administration was left in the
hands of Africans. These elite returnees and freed slaves
became magistrates, judges, lawyers, doctors, pastors, and
high administrative officials in the colonial government. This
occurred as early as 1850, before white settlers had even
begun their treks to Kenya, Zimbabwe, or Malawi. Thus,
West Africa led the way in educational advancement.
Today, West Indians and West Africans are employed in
East and Central Africa, filling the need for university-
trained people. Ghana, for instance, had twelve thousand
students in schools as early as 1860. By 1969-1970, Ghana
had more university graduates than Somalia, Kenya, Tanzania, Uganda, Malawi, Zambia, and Zimbabwe combined.
The early West African black rule on behalf of the British,
however, was not permanent. Soon after the malarial mosquito was identified and the swamps around these urban
areas were drained, whites of the British colonial service
moved into those important offices. Legislation requiring
British citizenship and education was enacted as a barrier to
Africans, and university education for Africans was down-
graded. In the areas where white residence was physically
easier (in the highlands of Kenya, Zambia, Malawi, and
Zimbabwe), African secondary education developed very
slowly. For instance, in 1970, white-ruled Zimbabwe had

about one-third as many Africans in secondary schools as in black-ruled Zambia, which had an African population of the same size. Yet white Zimbabwe boasted that it had the most advanced African education on the continent. This education was concentrated at the primary level. The number of educated Africans dropped off quickly at the secondary and university levels. Since independence in 1980, the government of Zimbabwe has removed all racial barriers, and schools are open to all citizens, regardless of color.

The Portuguese system of education grew the slowest of all. This should not be surprising because Portugal itself has been one of Europe's most illiterate nations. The school systems of Angola and Mozambique were oriented more to control of political dissidence than to education. A minority of the African children of school age were allowed into primary school. Fewer than two out of every one hundred pupils who began school were allowed to continue into the fourth grade. Portuguese was the language of instruction, and secondary education was virtually nonexistent. In 1960, under the Portuguese colonial government, fifty thousand students were enrolled in primary and secondary education. In 1981, under the independent Mozambiquan government, two million were enrolled—an increase of two thousand percent.

All of these colonial systems expanded African education at the primary level but neglected the expansion of secondary and university education. No one realized how quickly the winds of change would bring independence to Africa in the 1960s.

In 1960, at least eighty percent of the primary schools in Africa were mission schools. As a result, today the majority of African rulers of sub-Saharan African nations are Christian, even though a large proportion of the common people are Muslim. So close was the identification between school and church that the word for "church" in various southern African languages is "isikoli" (or a variation thereof) meaning "school." At the end of this period of early elite formation, there were small bands of educated people in the areas of greatest missionary contact, primarily along the coastline of Africa.

By the 1950s, the eve of African independence, there was a universal demand for access to education. This began the period of demand for education, and every African nation is in the middle of that movement now. This demand resulted from many factors, but the two most common are: First, the colonialists argued that whites should have special privileges including virtually all political power because they were educated. Education was held up as the golden key to power and self-rule for the future of the nation. As a result of this, many Africans demanded more schools. When the schools were not built rapidly enough and the demand for political independence escalated, the turmoil and struggle for independence began. Second, the rates of pay and job prestige in Africa were adopted largely from European and British standards. Thus, in many nations, a peasant may earn $30 per year; an urban worker with a grade school education may earn ten times that amount, or $300; the secondary or university graduate may earn even ten more, or $3,000. Thus, the way to wealth, health, and security is through the magic of education; most parents will struggle daily to place their children in school.

African development has achieved the greatest successes in education. All across the continent, children and adults are streaming to the school to obtain valuable knowledge for a better life and for personal advancement. At the time of the nations' independence, only about one-third of the primary school age group was found in the classroom. Twenty years later, almost two-thirds of that age group was in elementary classes, even though boys outnumbered girls three to two. In 1960, only sixteen percent of the adults were literate; by 1980, almost double that number could read and write. Similarly, at the time of independence, only about three percent of the high school age group could be found in the secondary classroom. By 1978, more than four times this amount, thirteen percent, were receiving a high school education. This priority for education is reflected in the African nations' budgets, which spend an average of fifteen percent of all public funds for schooling. Indeed, Ivory Coast spends over one-third of its national budget on education, and the following governments spend over twenty percent of their scarce public funding for education: Mali, Niger, Burundi, Lesotho, Swaziland, and Botswana.

Still, education remains valuable and scarce. Eighty-seven percent of high school-aged students find no place for continuing their education. Probably half of the continent's population has never been to school, and only one person in a hundred between the ages of twenty and twenty-four can enter the university.

THE DILEMMA OF EDUCATION IN INDEPENDENT AFRICA TODAY

Every independent nation in Africa is pouring scarce money into education, both to speed development and to fulfill the demands of the people. But education in and of itself does not ensure development. India, for example, one of the poor nations of the world, has no shortage of university graduates. Every African educational planner, therefore, is faced with the dilemma of making education appropriate to the needs of that nation.

What Goals Should the School Serve?

For the young pupil, education is the golden path to the good life. But the good life for the individual may not be good for the development of the country. Different national goals require different schools. A school curriculum changes radically if the nation's goals are changed from economic

(United Nations photo)

Independent governments have made literacy an important priority. National campaigns have been launched by many nations.

development to national integration or to creating national dignity and pride in one's national culture. Many nations are attempting to achieve all of these goals at once. The basic starting point for many educational programs were those of the colonial school.

Achieving pride in one's culture is an important goal. The colonial school did much to destroy this pride in African history, art, social organization, and other accomplishments. One colonial educator wrote in the 1920s about the kind of education that Africans needed:

> A fact of primary importance in African education is that outside Egypt there is nowhere any indigenous history . . . There is no 'African culture' . . . the African has no history . . . no recorded stages of development through which we can see some mental quality persisting. . . .[7]

In colonial Madagascar, which was controlled by the French, students were required to stand and recite *"Nos ancestres les Guals"* ("Our ancestors, the Gauls"). Now, the medium of instruction in the schools is the Malagasy language, and French is taught as a second language.

To compensate for this colonial misconception, the African educator now wants to include more instruction on African history; on local art, dance, and music; and on literature from African poets and novelists. But the African teacher, who was taught "universal" education—British history, the French Constitution, the works of Cicero and Shakespeare—without any African studies, is handicapped. The teacher must first learn and then struggle to introduce a new, genuinely African content into the curriculum.

The school also can help the nation build patriotism and identification with national development goals. Many nations believe it is important to transform the student's individual drive for success into commitment to the development of the nation. This process can be facilitated by teaching a common language such as English, French, or an indigenous tongue in the schools. This language enables the student to talk to others from a different background. This was the case for the early elite, who in a single secondary school of the colony came to know and trust one another in spite of diverse ethnic and linguistic backgrounds. This trust was used later in forging unity among African leaders in the independence movements.

The school can also train manpower for the tasks of economic development. Meeting together in Ethiopia in 1961, after most African nations had achieved independence, African educators formed a common educational policy:

> . . . in Africa, at its present level of development, the highest priority in education should be accorded to ensuring that an adequate proportion of the population receives at secondary and post-secondary levels the kinds of skills required for economic development.[8]

At this point, however, the priorities for economic development diverges. Should schooling prepare students for technical and engineering jobs, for agricultural occupations, or for private or public business?

Who Should Teach in African Schools?

This dilemma faces the nation that is short on teachers at various levels. Even highly educated Ghana still uses expatriate teachers in the universities. Foreign teachers, however, are expensive. They also are less likely to be committed to self-sacrifice and service to the nation. Should they be hired with scarce development funds? How important is it to have a professor with a doctorate to teach at the university, or a teacher with a college degree for secondary education?

What Buildings and Texts Are Needed for Learning?

The educator is forced to allocate scarce funds for buildings, equipment, services (films, slides, TV programs) and teachers. Each nation must decide what minimal facilities are needed. Should capital funds be invested in primary schools, secondary schools, or in the university? It is difficult to determine priorities.

Who Should Be Educated?

In 1978 about forty-four percent of all primary students in Africa were girls, while even fewer of the secondary students were girls. What should be the policy toward educating women? Most African families want their sons to go farther in school than their daughters. Should the schools accept that parental choice or should they insist on equal education? Tanzania, Zambia, Mozambique, Angola, and Zimbabwe have made concerted efforts to correct the imbalance of educational opportunities for girls. But the male dominance in political and managerial positions, which occurs in the United States, also occurs in Africa. Much intelligent woman-power is lost in that choice.

The educational administration must decide which economic and social classes should receive a good education. Of all children born in Africa in 1971, two-thirds remain illiterate because of the lack of schools, teachers, and budgets. Most of these children are in rural areas and/or are from poorer families. The child of the wealthier family has advantages that the poor child does not. These include: having less work to do in the home; hearing English or French spoken in the family; knowing which schools give better preparation for university work; having access to newspapers and magazines; being encouraged to complete lessons; and, not least, being able to pay fees or transportation costs for education. In Africa, as elsewhere, children of lawyers, teachers, politicians, businessmen, clergymen, and others who are well-to-do are getting more and better education at the secondary and university levels.

Many African governments are spending money for adult education, but this, too, is a difficult choice. The adult who is trained late in life has fewer productive years to give to the development of the nation.

What Educational Methods Should Be Used?

Just as there is controversy in the United States about which educational methods are best, Africa is searching for the best program as well. Do children need a nursery school program? Should classrooms have rigid discipline? Should there be greater personal freedom? Should the student follow a set curriculum or personal interests? How much education in history and literature is needed for the student who is training to be a tractor mechanic, an airline pilot, or an accountant? How much of this general education is useful for achieving development goals? Is a general and broad humanistic education a luxury in a poor, developing country?

What Can Be Done to Retain the Best Products of the Schools?

Africa already is suffering a "brain-drain" at two levels. First, in every small or rural community of Africa, the better-educated students are leaving for the city. The city provides the culture, the action, the bright lights, and the cosmopolitan social life that the school has taught its pupils to enjoy. The mass exodus of the educated creates many rural ghettos.

Second, there is a shortage of the critically needed, university-educated teachers and professionals. Various African elites have left their nations when their personal political fortunes changed. For example, many eastern Nigerians decided to stay in the United States after the defeat of their Biafran secession. Some Africans are leaving to work in Britain, France, Saudi Arabia, or in other African nations where salaries are better. With the high standard of living that elite Africans have learned to appreciate, and the low levels and rates of development in most of Africa, this draining away of educated talent hurts African development. Scarce African funds have been invested in the education of these young students. The nation needs their abilities.

How Can Education Be Linked to Manpower Needs?

Producing too many pharmacists when diesel repairmen are needed is an error that only a wealthy nation can afford. For this reason, African governments are attempting to plan the number of students who attend each level of the educational system. The first commitment is to primary education. Those who attended the 1961 educational conference in Ethiopia pledged to seek a full primary education for every African child by 1980. This goal has not been met because the economies and aid funds have failed to develop. Only a small proportion of the growing number of grade school graduates can continue on to high school, yet those who do not continue frequently are very much committed to the lifestyle of their teachers, to the city as a permanent home, and to the wealth and security they have read about or have been promised by their governments. They aspire to a lifestyle possible only in a highly developed nation, one which African nations cannot achieve in the students' lifetimes. The problem, therefore, is one that increasingly challenges African politicians. The government cannot meet all the expectations of these unemployed in the major African cities, who are increasingly dissatisfied and alienated.

Africa is committed to the rapid expansion of education. African governments are spending more for education than nations in Latin America or Asia. For this reason, determining a relevant education remains one of the most difficult problems yet to be untangled.

6

POLITICS IN AFRICA

Seek Ye First the Political Kingdom
Former President Kwame Nkrumah, Ghana

Most independent African nations are less than twenty-five years old. In 1950, there were only four independent nations in Africa: Egypt, Ethiopia (which never experienced any permanent colonization), Liberia (the outpost for black American returnees), and South Africa (created by a white minority). By 1962, twenty-five nations were independent—encompassing three-fourths of all African people. By 1980, there were forty-four independent African nations. These nations are struggling to find their own identity, their own self-hood in independence from the colonial "fatherland." But this is a difficult task. As President Kaunda of Zambia noted,

> No blessed amnesia steals over [the people] on the morning after Independence Day. They carry with them into the new society as part of their baggage the experience and heritage of their colonial past in spite of all their attempts to wipe the slate clean. Human nature is not, in the short run, changed by constitutional instruments.[9]

If, for most nations, politics is the art of the possible, politics in Africa may seem like the art of the impossible, so difficult are the problems. Most African nations gained political independence in the early 1960s, at the same time when prices were falling for African minerals and agricultural raw materials on the world market. This resulted in low

94

national incomes for the newly independent states. Furthermore, each new government was faced with a series of almost impossible problems: an electorate that had not exercised power under colonial paternalism, an educational system that had produced many persons with primary education but few secondary and university graduates, a shortage of foreign exchange with which to buy needed equipment, a demand from the people to Africanize the government immediately, a hungry populace that expected miracles of independence, and a population of diverse languages and ethnic groups who had been encouraged by the colonial officials to think of themselves as "tribesmen" instead of as Nigerians, Senegalese, or Tanzanians. Nevertheless, the colonial experience did sow the seeds of nationhood among the peoples who happened to live within the territory that was claimed as a colony by the European power.

COLONIAL POLITICS: 1880-1960

It was the colonial powers that had defined the boundaries of the new nations of Africa. These boundaries united different peoples of divergent languages and traditions. The major uniting factor among many such African peoples was their common opposition to white rule. This opposition was strong enough to galvanize African political interests to oppose the colonial governments. What were some of the specific changes wrought by colonial rule?

First was the welding of the diverse ethnic and language groups into a common body within the colony. Sometimes the boundary between two colonial powers divided people within the same language group. Colonial rule was felt initially in the form of military conquest. Once African opposition was defeated with rifles, gatling guns, and dynamite, the colonial administration frequently instituted the "hut tax" whereby a family paid taxes on each building in the village. Taxes were used in this way to prod the villager out of subsistence agriculture into wage labor for the colonial government or, in some colonies, for white settler farmers. The government needed money, and settlers were hard-pressed for cheap labor, so the laws requiring the "natives" to pay taxes in cash guaranteed both income for the government and a ready supply of labor for the roads, houses, mines, and farms. Thus, the villagers were counted, enrolled in the tax book of the white district commissioner, and made to serve the colonial state. Throughout each colony, the population gradually learned bits and pieces of a second common language—English, French, German, Portuguese, or Spanish.

In northern Nigeria, with one British official per hundreds of thousands of people scattered over many square miles, the colonial officials relied on the established Muslim Hausa state to collect their taxes. More than any other colonial power, the British purposely used indigenous political structures to rule. Their "indirect rule" used chiefs and village headmen as colonial middlemen to mediate between the people and the colonial government and companies. The Belgians, Portuguese, and French attempted a more direct rule, frequently bypassing the political rulers of the African society. The results of direct and indirect rule were very similar. The African village authorities became agents of the colonial regime and, in the process, lost respect in the eyes of the people. Many African societies had been ruled only by village leaders or headmen; they did not have chiefs or kings. Since these societies did not have a single seat of government or chief, they were termed "stateless societies" or "acephalous groups" (without a political head). In some cases, these societies were "given" chiefs by the colonial officers, even though the position had not existed previously. In other cases, where there were chiefs, the colonial power of the local settlers (as in Zimbabwe) intervened to choose or to help select new chiefs who would be more "understanding" of the colonial policies and officials. The final result of all

these changes was the degradation of many African traditional political leaders. It was not surprising, therefore, that
when the movements of independence arose among the
people in the 1940s and 1950s, the chiefs, traditional
counselors, elders, or their representatives were not the new
African political leaders. Instead, the leaders usually were
the rising young teachers, clergymen, and others who had
been educated. It was national, not local, self-determination
that these new African nationalist movements sought.

In addition to the colonial administration, new legal
systems were imposed by the colonial government. This
decreased the importance of the village judicial system for
the average person. In some countries, in case of a dispute
about a theft or an argument over an inheritance, the
aggrieved party could appeal the ruling of the chief to the
colonial district commissioner. This weakened and, in some
cases, replaced the traditional law.

New roads, automobiles, trucks, and railroads also united
peoples who had not previously known or worked with one
another. New lines of trade and influence were drawn to the
administrative centers of the colony and to the company
mines. New manufactured products were introduced to be
sold to the villager in exchange for cash crops (after taxes had
been paid).

The new schools brought young men and a few women of
different languages together. Out of this common experience
came those who later were to lead their nations to independence. Here, a whole generation of Africans was taught
that change was possible and desirable—change in levels of
wealth, in health care, disease control, and (though not
intended by the missionary or colonial official) in the
domination of one people by another. The seeds of the
African nationalist movements, which lay dormant under
colonial repression, were inadvertently sown by the missionaries and the colonial administrators themselves.

Most new schools, however, did not teach African history.

It was unknown to many of the teachers, and it was not considered worthy of study by colonial educators. In most instances, African history was considered uncivilized, and the school was a place for learning about "civilization"— meaning European history or world history, especially Western Europe and its expansion.

In Zimbabwe, for example, it was assumed by the white settlers that Africans could not possibly have built the large stone fortresses of the Rozwi Empire and that Africans were incompetent to rule themselves. Yet, the great stone enclosures and towers now have been proven to be of African construction. The "colonial mentality" resulted from such teaching and from the experience of racial discrimination. It has left deep scars in the African psyche. While the colonies in Africa did not have any experience as long and calamitous as the plantation slavery of the southern United States, the scars of prejudice and discrimination still may be seen in Africa. In South Africa, a magazine includes advertisements that promise skin-lightening cream to make African women "truly beautiful":

> Karoo morning, Karoo Night
> Makes You Lovely,
> Makes You Light—
>   the American Way.

No aspect of colonialism had such a deep or long-range effect on African societies as the practice of migrant labor. In the search for more and more cheap labor for plantations, mines, and railways, the companies and governments sent labor recruiters far and wide to seek workers. They advertised the ease of earning tax money, the new goods that wages could buy, and the excitement of town life. They even suggested that the proof of one's manhood could be found by working in mines and on plantations. This, combined with heavy taxes on all village populations, began the migratory labor system. As early as the 1920s, some parts of rural

Africa were virtually drained of able-bodied men who had left their homes to work for one or two years. As a result, some rural societies tottered dangerously. The absence of men meant no husbands for wives, no fathers for children, no ritual and political officials for the local religious and governmental structures, and insufficient labor to produce adequate food for the village. As a result, many rural areas began to import food from other regions or other countries. This imported food was purchased with the urban wages of the absent men. The labor shortages also meant great movements of laborers all over the continent: Kenyans travelled to Uganda to work; Upper Voltans migrated to Ghanaian farms; and Malawians, Zambians, Zimbabweans, and Tanzanians journeyed hundreds of miles to work in the mines of South Africa. Men going to work in another area had to learn new languages. Special languages, mixtures of European and African tongues, such as *"fanika lo"* or *Silapalapa*, were learned by the African miners in South Africa, Zaïre, Zimbabwe, and Zambia.

Not only were Africans used as migrant laborers, but they also were conscripted by the colonial powers during times of war in Africa and abroad. African troops fought in World Wars I and II, and Sengalese fought for the French in Vietnam.

Manufactured goods could be bought with the laborer's wage. As a result, in some remote villages of Africa today, women may be found raising chickens and cattle, caring for children, and building houses of mud and dung in age-old ways. But that same woman may mix her mortar in an enamel pan from Czechoslovakia; she may be dressed in a cloth printed in the Netherlands and wear plastic sandals from Hong Kong while she listens to world news on a Japanese transistor radio or writes to her husband with a British ball-point pen.

The result of the colonial contact, then was massive and rapid social change, which reached into the remotest corner of the colony. It was not surprising that the movements for self-determination and a better life took hold throughout the colony, not just in the urban centers but also in the village. When the demand for freedom was voiced in the 1950s, Britain, France, Belgium, and Portugal were astounded to see how universal was the demand, "Africa for the Africans." To their surprise, from the far corners of their colonies came the call for self-determination and "one-man-one-vote." It was said most clearly by the educated, in their clubs, unions, and political associations. But the movement was supported by the common people, who saw the possibility of change all about them but few ways for themselves or their children to have a part of that better life of health and wealth as independent, self-governing people.

INDEPENDENCE

The demand for independence came much sooner than the colonial powers expected. On the day of independence, no African nation had enough trained technicians, teachers, doctors, nurses, schools, hospitals, or money in the national treasuries to meet the needs of a new nation. One by one, the subjects of colonial regimes realized that they would not be allowed to achieve the education they needed as long as they did not have control of their government, schools, and the income from their labor. Among the people of the new nation, the expectations and demands for better life rose rapidly once the colonial rulers had gone. The demands for concrete improvements were high. But time was short. As one African president noted:

> Time is the scarcest of all Africa's resources. The preoccupation of the leaders of the new Africa is to purchase enough of it in which to establish a record of positive achievement which will give the people hope. To change the metaphor, they have got to get the roof on before the foundations crack—a task made formi-

dable by the anticlimactic atmosphere which is the inevitable aftermath of Independence.[10]

To hold these diverse and expectant groups together, each African government and its political parties campaigned for mass support by the people. The appeal frequently was based on united African loyalty against the former colonial master. This appeal had force even after independence because many companies, civil services, wholesale and retail stores were still foreign-dominated.

Among these foreigners were many middlemen, such as Indians, who had immigrated to Africa to become small store owners. In Central and East Africa, the best stores were owned and patronized by Europeans. The wholesale groceries, small shops, butcheries, and general stores that catered to African needs were operated by the Asians or Middle Easterners. The African traders, having little capital, peddled their wares in the marketplace or on the streets, loading their carts with bread, soft drinks, a selection of combs, matches, kerosene lamps, ball-point pens, and soap. Asians and Europeans were more readily given credit loans than Africans. This made it difficult for an African small businessman to get a shop. In some towns, there were even exclusive first-, second-, and third-class trading areas in which the shops were owned and operated by Europeans, Asians, and Africans, respectively. The presence of a wealthy foreign trading group caused resentment among many African peoples. Prices in the foreigners' stores frequently were high, much like in the United States where stores in the ghetto often charge high prices. The African people wanted to oust the foreigners from their posts of commercial and administrative privilege and power.

Most African countries have attempted to protect such foreign minorities from attack and from expropriation of their goods. In Kenya, for instance, a full ten years after independence, much of the real estate of the capital city of

(United Nations photo/J.P. Laffont)

In nations with weak or nonexistent democratic institutions, military rule or one-party states often follow the struggle for independence.

Nairobi was still in the hands of the Asian minority, an intolerable situation for many African peoples. This concern was not just a symbolic issue, because high profits were flowing out of the country. As a result, nations such as Kenya passed legislation requiring that small shops and companies be operated by Kenyan citizens. Some have labeled this "racial discrimination" against Europeans and Asians. In most instances, it is not racial discrimination but national discrimination against foreigners who refuse to become citizens of the nation.

In Uganda, this feeling against people who ran businesses in the country but kept their homes, bank accounts, and citizenship in foreign nations resulted in the eviction of many persons of Asian origin, especially those of Indian extraction, from the country. It was true that many such business families were illegally sneaking their profits out of the country, but it also was true that many Ugandans of Asian origin were loyal citizens of the country. Many had been born in the country. As a result, many fled to Canada, the United States, and the United Kingdom. Rationalization for such an attack on the Ugandan Asians was made possible by their wealth in contrast to most Ugandans, their long-time protection and assistance by the colonial government, and their racial separateness. Some also violated the country's laws by keeping profits in foreign banks instead of in the country. This was particularly frowned upon because the goal of the new governments is to use the national income for the direct benefit of the citizens of that nation, not for foreign individuals and companies.

ONE-PARTY STATES

Many African nations have responded to the first decade of self-determination with *de facto* one-party governments and, in several cases, military rule. Outsiders may see the one-party state as dictatorial rule, the elimination of opposition. Single party rule of the nation has developed for several reasons. First, independence from the colonial power usually was won by the action of a single party representing all those Africans united against the alien Europeans. The first president of each African nation, the "father of his country," belonged to that one party. It would be difficult for another party to rise so soon against a party that could claim it had won independence and that its leader was the father of the nation. These "fathers" of African nations may not want to step down or to submit to a partisan election. Such elections, many Africans feel, may be a luxury that a nation can enjoy once some social and political unity has been welded together by common history. During the divide-and-rule era of colonialism, this unity was not achieved. The 1983 elections in Nigeria were contested by several political parties, as were the 1980 elections in Zimbabwe.

Second, these African nations have a dual goal—development and distribution of the wealth from development. There are, however, too few persons with the education and technical training to meet the needs of development. Government, industry, and foreign companies compete to employ the educated men and women. With so few well-qualified persons for public office and administration, a two-party system is wasteful because it requires two sets of qualified persons to compete for the same offices. There is also a desperate need for continuity in office in many of those countries where the chaos of change from colonial to African rule means discontinuity of policy and administration. Finally, every African nation is beset by problems of disunity and national integration. Diverse interests in some areas have caused rival ethnic and language groups to contend for power, money, and jobs.

In some cases, foreign governments have attempted to exploit disunity for their own interests. The result of this disunity in Nigeria was the civil war which developed when comparatively wealthy eastern Nigeria (Biafra) attempted to secede. The Katanga Province of Zaïre also attempted to secede with its mineral wealth. Every African government is anxious to prevent such dangerous splintering and disrupting dissension. Those who talk of splintering, of secession, or of divergent policies may be regarded as traitors who are more interested in their own bank accounts than in the development of the whole nation. Sometimes such charges are just. In other cases, a charge is made by selfish politicians who are themselves lining their pockets with public money. The threat of disunity, therefore, is a serious one. One answer is the single-party state. An advantage of the single-party system is that no particular social class or ethnic group can form a new party for its own particular interest. Instead, everyone is forced to work with everyone else, including the masses of the nation. The disadvantage is that whenever special powerful interests gain power over that single party, the common people may have no alternative voice. For this reason some nations such as Zimbabwe have not yet legislated against all other parties but have stated that it is their hope and goal to achieve single-party rule. Where only one party is allowed by law, the democratic process still is possible by allowing opposition within the party.

Such a system is used in the CCM (Chama Cha Mapinduzi), which is the one legal party of Tanzania. The nation is divided into over one hundred election districts. In each district, a committee of citizens screens all nominations to select the two best qualified candidates. Anyone may be nominated with only twenty-five signatures on a petition. The citizens' committee holds election debates in which the two chosen candidates speak and answer questions. No discussion of racial, ethnic, or religious issues takes place, and each candidate must speak in Swahili, the single national language, instead of any local language used by one particular group. Clearly, the Tanzanian system has preserved democratic choice within a single party. In the 1975 elections, less than fifty percent of the incumbents were reelected.

In all elections since 1965, cabinet ministers have been defeated by the voters at the local level, and representatives with strong local support have survived reelection.

PRESSURE FROM SPECIAL INTEREST GROUPS

Regardless of the mechanism to preserve democracy or participation by all citizens, most African governments are attempting to hold together a fragile balance of diverse groups of people who fear they will lose power. Six common African social groups are: the older "freedom-fighters," many of whom had little education or training, but who won independence; the small elite group of well-educated people who are now at the top of the government; the growing number of younger and highly educated men and women from the expanded secondary schools and universities; the thousands of young people called "school-leavers," who are unable to go beyond primary school (frequently they are unemployed and very active in the militant youth leagues of the political party); urban workers with little or no education; and the masses of subsistence farmers, peasants, and cash farmers in the countryside. The last group constitutes the largest part of the population and frequently has benefited least from independence. Across Africa we find these various social groups in conflict with one another, even though it is not reported in the newspapers.

The unrest and contention among these various interest groups, especially in the capital cities and industrial centers, are a threat to stability. These problems also hinder long-term economic development. As the unrest grows louder and threatens to become open rioting and even revolution, a common phenomenon appears in Africa—the development of military rule. By the 1980s, a majority of the African nations were under military rule, and at least thirty of the independent nations had experienced a military intervention of some form. Some say that the military only seek to ensure their own wealth and power. Others contend they are representing conservative interests, as they frequently do in Latin America. The late Kwame Nkrumah, former leader of Ghana, said the military is "arrogant, ambitious, elite, [and] imperialist-trained." The justifications for military rule in Africa vary according to the situations and the spokesmen. The military leadership claims that disorder is imminent, that the democratic process has broken down, and that the civilian governmental leaders have become corrupt. Only one fact is clear: the military has the guns with which to force its will on a nation, even when it is a small army by Western standards. In several cases, as in Nigeria, Africa's most populous nation, the military has turned the power back to elected (or appointed) civilian officials. In a few cases, the military leader has attempted to found a new popularly-supported political party and to stand for election in order to become legitimate. Military rule, more than single-party rule, stifles opposition and may crush dissent. More important than the form of government, however, is whether development occurs, whether incomes, health care, and numbers of schools increase. If they do not, any government—military or civilian, multi-party or single-party—will not be able to contain the demands of the people.

Because Africa has many votes in the United Nations and great potential economic power, many foreign nations have considerable interest in who governs African countries. To keep a leader in power who is friendly to their political and economic interests, some foreign powers will provide military and economic assistance for deposing unfriendly leaders. Thus, Israel assisted Idi Amin to stage a coup against Milton Obote, the democratically elected prime minister of Uganda. The Soviet Union has provided military assistance to a number of countries and liberation groups. France has intervened in Chad, the Central African Republic, and other former colonies with money, arms, and soldiers. The United States has assisted unpopular leaders such as General

Mobutu of Zaïre to stay in power and to resist change and participation of diverse interest groups of the society in the government of the country. This continuing intervention and manipulation of African affairs by outside "superpowers," such as Britain, France, the USSR, and the United States, breeds the belief among many African people that the avowed interest of the West in democracy, majority rule, and freedom, and of the Eastern bloc in rule by the workers or people, are just convenient slogans and ideologies to disguise the East-West global conflict. As a result, there is a new drive in Africa in the 1980s for "Africa for the Africans," for freedom from foreign manipulation, wherever it is found.

ONE AFRICA?

The dream of a powerful united Africa has inspired men—black and white—through the centuries. Pioneer American and West Indian blacks—such as Marcus Garvey, Edward Blyden, Bishop H.M. Turner, Casely Hayford, and others—wanted a union of all black peoples in Africa and the West. Cecil Rhodes wanted to unite African colonies under the British Union Jack. More realistically, the first eight black independent nations of Africa met in 1958 to seek pan-African unity on a number of problems. The nations were Ghana, Ethiopia, Liberia, Sudan, Libya, Egypt, Morocco, and Tunisia. After many negotiations and false starts, the independent black African nations founded the Organization of African Unity (OAU) in 1963 to solve common problems and to speak with one voice to the world and in the United Nations. The OAU has served to negotiate potential crises between various African governments and supported the African liberation movements in Zimbabwe, Angola, Mozambique, Guinea-Bissau, Namibia, and South Africa. But the need for development funds, border and political disputes, divergent economic interests, as well as the ties of the African nations to the former colonial powers continue to undermine the strength of the OAU. Thus, some French-speaking nations continue to receive foreign assistance from France, to use French companies and teachers, and to orient trade to other French-speaking countries. The English-speaking nations continue to have special ties in trade, language, and politics with the British Commonwealth. Others, such as Mali, have struck a more diversified course. Thus, African unity grows slowly. It flounders on the compromises and problems each nation faces in its search for development, personnel, and assistance.

CONCLUSION

It is easy to become pessimistic about African politics. Until 1983, there was civil war in Chad, where there is an Eritrean liberation movement to free the northern territory from the rest of the nation. In the 1960s a disastrous civil war erupted after the Biafran secession from Nigeria, Africa's most populous nation. A flood of military *coup d'etats* have come on the heels of freedom from colonial rule. The African liberation movements' drive for freedom in South Africa and Namibia have been stalled since the late 1970s.

But Westerners should not conclude that Africa is a "lost cause." Rather, we should remember the first decades of the American Continental Congress, when the nation's treasury was empty after the costly war that had disrupted trade. In those days, the Congress faced the threats of unemployed soldiers in the streets of Philadelphia who demanded their pay "or else." The Congress quickly moved to famous Nassau Hall in rural Princeton, New Jersey, to escape the threat of disruption and military overthrow and in order to conduct their deliberations in peace.

On the positive side of the balance sheet, we must note that, by and large, African nations have found hope and exhilaration in self-determination and in freedom from racist colonialism. Many nations have succeeded in establishing constitutional rule of law with equal rights for all. They have established a spirit of cooperation in working to build schools and hospitals, to staff classrooms and governments, and to open new agricultural cooperatives. They have pioneered broad-scale experimentation in new types of communities, collective-farms, and cooperative villages. They have built new roads, factories, railroads, dams, and opened new farmlands. They have demonstrated independence from any power, be it capitalist or communist. They have established new channels of cooperation and common action among nations that thirty years ago had little or no contact. They have built new hopes for change and development in their peoples. Some nations have built strong popularly supported political parties. They have accomplished much in spite of the terrible twenty years of economic slide in the price paid on world markets for their products and a high inflation rate in the prices Africa pays for foreign products.

If the problems of development are too overwhelming and the capability of the governments to meet the needs of the people is not great enough, there may be more unrest and disorder, because "Wood already touched by fire is not hard to set alight." (Ghanaian Proverb)

In this context, the powerful Western nations need to remember that the development of African countries is partly their responsibility. The prices Western nations pay for African commodities, the import duties levied against African products, and the aid and assistance provided to these new governments may combine to determine the economic foundation on which the social and political structure of Africa can grow.

7

SOUTHERN AFRICA:
A CASE STUDY

A crisis exists in southern Africa which may involve the entire world. The crisis has been created by the continuing rule of a powerful minority of whites over the black people of South Africa and Namibia, the only two African nations remaining under white minority rule. This minority rule denies the black majority their rights to "life, liberty, and the pursuit of happiness," cherished values throughout the world. In South Africa, racism, economic and political oppression, and social injustice are legally determined by the Constitution. A sad irony in South Africa is that the white minority claims to abide by Western, Christian values as it extends and strengthens the racist system that denies African people their basic human rights.

ABROGATION OF HUMAN RIGHTS

Africans have no right to vote now and are not represented in the South African Parliament. Political control by the whites (or "Europeans" as whites are labeled) was extended in order to protect their economic interests. Today, this control reaches into every phase of African life. The meaning of white supremacy is clearly seen by contrasting certain South African laws in force today with portions of the *Universal Declaration of Human Rights of the United Nations:*

United Nations Article 13: "Everyone has the right to freedom of movement . . . within the borders of each State."

In South Africa: Any municipal council may at any time, require all African residents in the municipal area who do not own land and are not employed there to leave the area, although they have resided there continuously for fifty years.

The Minister of Justice may prohibit any person from being in any area, for such period as he chooses to specify, if he decides that such person is "promoting feelings of hostility between whites and nonwhites."

A visiting African-American walking in a street in a city in South Africa may be stopped by a policeman who believes that "he in appearance obviously is a member of an aboriginal race or tribe in Africa," and be required to produce his Reference Book (identification passbook). He will be presumed to be an African and therefore liable to arrest for failure to produce it, unless he proves that "he is not in fact and is not generally accepted as" a member of an aboriginal race or tribe of Africa.

United Nations Article 23: "Everyone has the right to work, to free choice of employment, to just and favourable conditions of work and to protection against unemployment. . . . Everyone has the right to form and join trade unions for the protection of his interests."

In South Africa: A labor officer may, at any time, cancel the employment of an African who works in town, no matter how long he has been employed, even though his employer opposes the cancellation. It is unlawful for an African worker to take part in a strike for any reason whatsoever.

United Nations Article 26: "Everyone has the right to education."

In South Africa: No school for the education of African children may be conducted anywhere in South Africa unless it is registered by the government. The Minister of African Education has unfettered discretion to refuse to register it if he believes that its existence is not in the interests of the African people.

United Nations Article 16: "Men and women of full age, without any limitation due to race, nationality, or religion, have the right to marry and to found a family."

In South Africa: If a white South African lawfully marries a "coloured" (racially mixed) woman abroad, the marriage is void and of no effect in South Africa. Marriages between whites and blacks are illegal.

United Nations Article 16: "Everyone has the right to peaceful assembly and association.

In South Africa: It is unlawful for a white person and a non-white person to drink a cup of tea together in a cafe anywhere in South Africa unless they have obtained a special permit to do so or unless the establishment has been declared an "international" eating place.

Unless he or she has obtained a special permit, an African professor delivering a lecture at a white club, which has invited him or her to do so, commits a criminal offence.

United Nations Article 19: "All are equal before the law and are entitled without any discrimination to equal protection of the law."

In South Africa: No African is entitled to hold title to land anywhere in white South Africa; nor is it the intention of the present government ever to grant such right to the African.

United Nations Article 19: "Everyone has the right to freedom of opinion and expression."

In South Africa: The South African Publications Control Board functions to prevent the showing of any educational documentary film which expresses approval of racial integration or disapproval of discrimination based on race and color.

A white man who tells a group of Africans that the apartheid (racial segregation) laws are unjust and should be disobeyed is guilty of an offense.

According to the law of South Africa, "communism" is, among other things, "any doctrine or scheme which aims at the encouragement of feelings of hostility between European and non-European races of the Republic, the consequence of which are calculated to further the achievement" of the object of "bringing about any social change in the Republic by the threat of unlawful acts or omissions."[11]

APARTHEID

This official policy, which is practiced in South Africa, is called *apartheid* (pronounced apart-hate) and means "separateness." South African whites are attempting to build separate social and political systems for the Africans, for the so-called "coloured" (people of mixed ancestry), and for persons of Asian descent, while preserving control of their labor to serve white interests. This official policy of apartheid means separate development of the races, separate housing areas, separate schools, public telephones, railway coaches, universities, and public facilities. However, complete separation, pure apartheid, is impossible to practice.

WHITE AND BLACK CONDITIONS IN SOUTH AFRICA

	White	Black
Percent of Population*	16	72
Percent of Land Reserved	87	13
Distribution of Income (1977)	64%	26%
Average monthly wage in mining (1979)	$1,056	$175
in manufacturing (1980)	$1,273	$308
Government expenditure per pupil in school (1978-1979)	$833	$82

*Asian and Coloured are 12% of the population and receive 10% of the income.

Source: Africa Fund, *Southern Africa Perpectives,* "South African Fact Sheet," New York, 1981.

These racial groups are tied together by the white need for cheap labor to run the industries and mines, to clean and cook in white homes, to garden, and to care for white children. African laborers work in white areas during the day; African domestic servants live in white areas day and night. This reveals the real keystone of South African policy—white supremacy, not apartheid. Apartheid regulations may be altered to allow a black worker to have a job which was formerly reserved for whites only. The regulation may simply raise the barrier and reclassify the job as "black" instead of "white." This does not change the fact that the whites control the best jobs, for blacks may not take jobs superior to whites except under very special circumstances. In fact, when apartheid and white supremacy come into conflict, apartheid gives way. For example, a white suburb of Johannesburg was to be declared "white by night"—that is, at night all domestic servants were to live in separate African housing areas outside the white city. The white people in this suburb, however, wanted their servants to stay on the premises in their servants' quarters behind the white home because they were needed when the white family entertained or required a babysitter in the evening. The order of "white by night," which would have been a strict interpretation of apartheid, was not enforced. Former Prime Minister John Vorster expressed the government's view in these words:

> The fact of the matter is we need them (Africans) because they work for us, but after all we pay them for their work. . . . But the fact that they work for us can never entitle them to claim political rights. Not now, not in the future, under no circumstances can we grant them those political rights in our own territory, neither now nor ever.

HOMELANDS

In order to preserve white supremacy and enforce apart-

(United Nations photo)

South Africa's "Homeland" policy defines many blacks as foreigners, thus denying them rights of citizenship.

heid, the South African government has created African homelands, formerly called *bantustans,* designed to be "independent states" within South Africa. These homelands are on the thirteen percent of the land reserved for African use, and most of them have very limited agricultural potential. They contain almost none of the rich diamonds, gold, and other precious metals, and none of the wealthy cities and industrial centers. They are not served by the excellent white South African transportation system, and they are simply scattered pieces of land within South Africa. Not one is a single geographic entity.

Millions of Africans—mostly older men and women, children, widows, the chronically sick, and the unemployed or unemployable—are legally defined as foreigners in the Republic of South Africa. Stripped of their rights as citizens, they are "deported" from the urban areas to these homelands. The removals implement the principle of apartheid, while preserving the needed labor supply for white industry and commerce. To speed up the establishment of white industries near the homelands, the government has given cheap loans, tax concessions, and rail rebates to industries that locate away from the present urban industrial areas and near the supply of cheap African labor in the homelands. Many Africans have been uprooted and ordered out of the areas where they have lived for generations. They are sent to homelands arbitrarily selected for their ethnic group. Many find these lands unfamiliar in climate, land, and growing conditions. They must build houses and reestablish a way of life under very inadequate and difficult conditions. As early as fifteen years ago a white woman member of the South African Parliament, who has been a lone critical voice in that body, said this about the resettlement policy which continues in the mid-1980s:

> . . . the mass removal of people in South Africa is a violence, . . . the thousands upon thousands of Afri-

(United Nations photo/Milton Grant)

Mfanafuthi Johnstone Makatini represents the African National Congress (ANC) before the UN General Assembly. The ANC resistance movement fights government policies in South Africa.

cans in resettlement areas, leading hopeless and help-
less lives of poverty and unemployment is a violence,
the very way in which those removals have taken place
is a violence. . . .[12]

The homeland policy has created nine of these territories,
and South Africa has declared four of them to be "independent nations." They are the Transkei, Venda, Bophuthatswana,
and the Ciskei. All, however, remain under the ultimate
control of the South African government, and all are totally
dependent on South Africa economically. No nation of the
world, other than South Africa, has recognized the "independence" of these African homelands. They have been
created in order to respond to the world's criticism of the
apartheid policies of South Africa, but most knowledgeable
black South Africans denounce both the creation of these
homelands and the Africans who have been persuaded to
govern them.

LIBERATION MOVEMENTS

The African National Congress (ANC), the leading black
political party, refuses to accept this division of the country
into small, vulnerable, dependent states and calls rather for a
unified South Africa where all the races share in the
government and in the wealth of the nation. As long ago as
1955, the ANC, the South African Indian Congress, the
South African Coloured People's Organization, and the
Congress of Democrats adopted the Freedom Charter,
which summarized the goals in the preamble:

*We, the People of South Africa, declare for all our
country and the world to know:*

- that South Africa belongs to all who live in it, black
  and white, and that no Government can justly claim
  authority unless it is based on the will of all the
  people;

- that our people have been robbed of their birthright
  to land, liberty and peace by a form of government
  founded on injustice and inequality;

- that our country will never be prosperous or free
  until all our people live in brotherhood, enjoying
  equal rights and opportunities;

- that only a democratic State, based on the will of all
  the people, can secure to all their birthrights without
  distinction of colour, race, sex or belief;

- and, therefore, we the people of South Africa, black
  and white together—equals, countrymen and brothers—adopt this Freedom Charter. And we pledge
  ourselves to strive together, sparing neither strength
  nor courage, until the democratic changes set out
  here have been won.

Many years of unfulfilled hope for peaceful change in
South Africa have resulted in the decision by many Africans
that only force will win independence, economic justice, and
racial equality. Some leaders of the liberation movements
compare their struggle to the American War of Independence,
when British colonial rule of America was defeated. Many of
the leaders of these movements have received their formal
education in Christian missions and Western universities.
They have lived overseas in nations without colonial or
apartheid rule; they have met with United Nations commit-
tees; they have experienced some of the freedom that they
cherish for their own people. Decades of pleading their case
to the local whites, to colonial powers, and, finally, to the
United Nations failed. In the early 1960s, the decision was
made to fight for independence and freedom.

Africans have resisted white dominance since it began
over three hundred years ago. When the white South
African government of 1948 initiated the official policy of
apartheid, resistance by blacks took nonviolent forms, such
as bus boycotts, burning of Reference Books, work stoppages,

demonstrations, and formal written protests. After 1960, however, when the white government ordered police to shoot hundreds of blacks joining such nonviolent protests throughout South Africa, the ANC and the Pan Africanist Congress (PAC), both major liberation movements, concluded that armed struggle was necessary to achieve freedom and equality. In recent years, acts of sabotage against military offices, police and government administrative buildings, and other strategic places, such as a petroleum storage plant, have occurred regularly. During this time, the white government has doubled and re-doubled its military and police budget, has instituted a universal draft for white males, and now boasts the largest and best-equipped military force in Africa. The liberation struggle is supported primarily by those independent nations who are members of the Organization of African Unity, by the United Nations, by Western and Eastern countries that support human rights and political freedom, and by churches, labor unions, liberation support groups, political parties, and individuals in the United States, Canada, Europe, and elsewhere. The moral, financial, military, and material assistance received from these sources is vital to the struggle being waged by the African people within their country.

UNITED STATES TIES TO SOUTH AFRICA

Members of the African liberation movements assert that Americans are too complacent about American partnership with the white South African government. Specifically, they note that representatives of the United States government cooperate with white South Africans, especially in marketing their products, which are made profitable by the low black wages. Furthermore, they point to the special preferential sugar quota given to the South African sugar companies and to the growing flood of white American tourists who add more dollars to the white-controlled economy and who willingly live and eat in racially segregated facilities.

Worst of all, many Africans feel, are the growing investments of American corporations in South Africa. The profits on these investments and on the growing South Africa-United States trade are drawn from the cheap labor of Africans. In addition, the presence of these firms and taxes paid by them give strength to the white-controlled economy and confidence to the whites to proceed with their white-supremacy policies. As one South African businessman put it, "So long as United States banks and business back us, we can go ahead."

Not only do American firms strengthen the economy generally, but American industries in South Africa are involved in the critical production of motor vehicles and computers, and there are American-owned oil refineries as well. American imported equipment—including computers and nuclear reactors—are used by the South African government to resist the movements for change from the Africans. Some American businessmen argue that offering jobs to Africans, even in segregated positions and at poverty-level wages, is a positive contribution to the African peoples. These Americans say that by offering jobs to South African blacks and by attempting to bring desegregation into the work place, they are achieving more good than they would by leaving South Africa in protest. Furthermore, they argue, other foreign companies would take their place if they left South Africa.

Critics of this point of view argue that African employees of United States firms comprise less than two percent of the total African labor force in the country, so the effect on local unemployment is small and that these corporations do support the apartheid system by giving it important military and strategic technology, by paying the government taxes, and by providing it with a certain legitimacy.

AN ALTERNATIVE TO WHITE SUPREMACY: NON-RACIALISM IN SOUTHERN AFRICA

What would happen if blacks came to power? Let us examine the case of Zambia, formerly Northern Rhodesia. This rich copper area attracted white miners and settlers from South Africa. It was ruled by the British and finally became independent Zambia under a black leadership in 1964.

President Kenneth Kaunda and other political leaders of Zambia personally experienced the full force of racial discrimination in colonial Northern Rhodesia. President Kaunda was once "frog-marched" out of a drugstore and called a "black-skinned nigger" by local whites when he dared to buy a book. Kaunda recalls another incident when he entered a cafe to buy sandwiches:

> On asking me what I wanted, she repeated that 'boys' were not served at that counter. I repeated in my turn that I was not a 'boy.' (Kaunda was age 33 at that time.) At this point I was dragged out of the cafe by my clothes by a European man. . . . Five other white men joined him in attacking us and we defended ourselves.[13]

When the men were taken to the police station, the white superintendent of police called Kaunda and his friend "cheeky niggers" and berated them for having the audacity to describe a European lady as a "woman."

In spite of this, when independence came, Kaunda and his government were happy to choose as a Zambian delegation to the United Nations Special Committee two Africans, one white and one Asian, symbolizing Zambia's commitment to non-racism. Furthermore, Kaunda writes this about whites who choose to stay in Zambia:

> We recognize that Zambia will be all the richer for the wealth and variety of human types within it. . . . We are not interested in white *Africans,* it is white *Zambians*

we value—Europeans who are committed to our country and its future, loyal to our State, serving according
to their gifts and providing a distinctive colour in the
rich tapestry of our national life.[14]

This hope for multi-racialism in Zambia, Zimbabwe, and
other African nations is supported by official government
non-racial policies, the Constitution, Bills of Rights, and
guarantees of the equality of all citizens in the eyes of the law.
No longer are advancement and privilege determined by race
but by ability, training, and contribution to the nation.

It is not surprising that the white press of South Africa
does not report the successes of these non-racial black
nations, such as Kenya, Zambia, and Zimbabwe. Instead,
whites in South Africa and even in the United States read far
more about those instances of failure of non-racism. They
are told that black racism is the rule instead of the exception.

NAMIBIA

Namibia (formerly South West Africa) was once under
the control of the South African government as a mandate
from the League of Nations. In 1966, the United Nations
declared that South Africa had forfeited its mandate because,
through the apartheid policy, it had failed to govern the
territory in the best interests of its inhabitants. The United
Nations demanded that South Africa give the territory back
to the United Nations, but in reality, South Africa has
maintained control of Namibia. In June 1971, the International Court of Justice declared that South Africa's occupation of Namibia was illegal. This has been to no avail.
Namibia is wealthy in diamonds, copper, lead, zinc, and
precious metals, as well as the largest known uranium
deposits in the world. South Africa wants to control this
wealth. The International Court's opinion denies South
Africa the legal right to allow international companies to
exploit Namibian workers and the area's natural resources.

South Africa, however, is eager to maintain those mining profits and to protect the seventy-five thousand whites who live there. Namibia also serves South Africa as a buffer state. If Namibia had an independent black government, the security of the apartheid system in South Africa would be endangered even more.

The Southwest African Peoples' Organization (SWAPO) has been waging guerrilla war from Angola into northern Namibia for more than fifteen years. To counter this force, South African troops have conducted raids into the southern provinces of Angola, an independent nation, to attack SWAPO's military bases. Thousands of Angolan villagers have been killed during these raids. SWAPO's military struggle is complemented by its political efforts in the United Nations to call for universal sanctions against South Africa for its continued illegal and oppressive presence in Namibia. By the early 1980s, the international community had not taken decisive action to force South Africa to withdraw from Namibia.

Although African leaders continue to offer an open door to negotiations with the white government of South Africa, they have received no serious indication that the whites wish to negotiate. The whites possess overwhelming military power and a desire, above all else, to preserve their economic privilege, their standard of living, their "way of life," and their control over the black majority. White unwillingness to tolerate change has caused an escalating conflict between Africans and whites across the whole of southern Africa. Such a conflict will not leave the rest of the nations of the world untouched, for most of the world has a stake in the outcome of that struggle.

SOUTH AFRICA ON THE ATTACK

The South African government realizes that its fight to preserve white supremacy will be difficult in light of the push for multi-racial equality that now exists in South Africa's neighbors: Zimbabwe, Botswana, Zambia, Mozambique, and Angola. Therefore, South Africa has gone on the attack against anyone regarded as an enemy.

First of all, the South African government attacks surrounding independent African nations who might support the liberation movements. Thus, arms, equipment, and money are provided for anyone who will undermine the governments of Mozambique, Zimbabwe, Angola, and even small Lesotho. In Mozambique, for example, South Africa is actively supporting anti-government individuals and movements who will attack isolated farmers, communities, government clinics and agricultural stations, and bus riders or motorists on lonely highways. Regional "destabilization" is backed with economic attacks as well: These include holding up goods passing through South Africa to and from these countries, blowing up oil storage depots in these countries, and charging higher customs and rail costs on goods from these countries. South Africa also commissions assassins to kill exiled South Africans in Mozambique, Lesotho, Angola, and Zimbabwe. In all these activities, South Africa seeks to distract the attention of the world from its racial policies and to cripple the genuine efforts of these surrounding nations to build economically healthy and secure multi-racial states, which would be an embarrassment to South Africa, for whom multi-racial cooperation is "impossible."

South Africa is also on the attack in Europe and the United States in a variety of ways. Millions of South African rands are spent for a variety of intelligence and propaganda efforts, including very slickly produced tourism films, filmstrips, and teaching materials distributed free to United States schools. Many publications, including *South African Panorama,* are sent free to school and university libraries. Free and inexpensive trips to South Africa are given to American community and political leaders, such as congressmen, senators, governors, corporation heads, and prominent doctors and lawyers. The aim of these trips is to win these Americans over to the cause of racial segregation and apartheid. In addition, South Africa engages in illegal activities in the United States, including spying on South African black and white students living and studying here in order to report them for speaking out against apartheid or even reading books or keeping posters that are banned in South Africa. In addition, South Africans have bragged publicly in Europe that they invested $25 million United States dollars to help defeat Senator Dick Clark of Iowa, the chairman of the Senate Africa Subcommittee, who opposed United States ties to South Africa. In 1982, a number of South African government representatives and visitors appeared in the Michigan district of Congressman Howard Wolpe, the Democratic Chairman of the House Africa Subcommittee, urging Americans not to support Wolpe's re-election because of his opposition to United States ties with South Africa. South Africa's own official government investigation committee has openly reported on the illegal giving of over $11 million to a pro-South African Michigan newspaper magnate who wanted to purchase the now-defunct *Washington Star* newspaper, giving the South Africans a strong, friendly voice to influence the United States government.

THE WESTERN RESPONSE

The Western nations have traditionally had strong ties with South Africa because of the large market for industrial goods there, the key minerals and metals supplied from South Africa, and the historical ties of South Africa with Western Europe and the United States during World War II. (Nigerians, Senegalese, Sudanese, Zambians, Kenyans, Congolese, and others also died for the Western Allies during World War II.) The West also has both historical and current interests in the rest of Africa as well. For instance, by 1983, the United States had more trade with Nigeria than with South Africa, a reversal of the earlier South African predominance. Britain, too, has a special interest in the Nigerian market and actually has changed certain foreign policies for fear of losing Nigeria as a market for British goods and as a source of petroleum. Thus, increasingly, the Western nations are learning the long-term interests in trade with all of Africa may be more important than the short-term advantage of the South African markets and minerals.

In the 1970s and 1980s, many organizations and individuals across the United States have sought to bring peaceful pressure on South Africa for ending its apartheid policy. In the face of South African intransigence, literally dozens of city councils, state legislatures, national labor unions, and religious organizations have called on United States corporations to stop supporting South Africa with taxes, technology, and friendship. When these companies have failed to act accordingly, various state, local, and national agencies have sold the stockholdings in those companies in South Africa and have taken their monies out of banks making loans to South Africa. Because of the good profits made on cheap African labor in the South African Republic and the long history of some companies there (Ford Motor Company was established there over sixty years ago), most of the companies have resisted the pressures.

Pressure is growing on Western Europe, Japan, and the United States to disassociate themselves from South African racism. The situation in South Africa grows more and more violent each year. In 1983 there were over one hundred incidents of armed attacks by African peoples in South Africa against property, the military, and the police. More and more, the Western democracies will be put to the test. South Africa calls for active support of its policies and programs in the name of maintaining a "bulwark of Christian nationalism against Communism" on a rapidly-changing continent, where many strategic minerals are at stake. The independent black nations respond that because of their democratic principles of majority rule the West cannot side with racism, repression, and profit-making in South Africa, the only nation in the world in which legalized racial discrimination is enshrined in the Constitution. Principles and profits are at stake in a struggle in which the common peoples of the villages and towns of South Africa must suffer. This cauldron of southern Africa will claim the attention of citizens of Western nations for years to come.

8

AFRICAN CULTURE: CONTINUITY AND CHANGE

VILLAGE PHILOSOPHY: THE PROVERB

The natural idiom of village philosophy is the proverb. In Rwanda and Burundi, they say, "Proverbs are the daughters of experience." And frequently, the experience bears a moral for the listener. The following are good examples:

> When a man is coming toward you, you need not say: "Come here." (Ghana)

Or for the family:

> The ruin of a nation begins in the homes of its people. (Ghana)

At other times, the proverbs are used to poke fun at those who seek wealth or who are too proud:

> A man with too much ambition cannot sleep in peace. (Chad)
>
> A man's wealth may be superior to him. (Cameroon)
>
> A wealthy man will always have friends. (Cameroon)

Throughout, the proverbs call for integrity, honesty, and candor:

> The teeth are smiling, but is the heart? (Zaïre)
>
> He who cannot dance will say: "The drum is bad." (Ghana)
>
> He who is free of faults will never die. (Zaïre)

Many problems addressed in proverbs are familiar in Western literature such as Aesop's fables.

> You do not teach the paths of the forest to an old gorilla. (Zaïre)

> Two birds disputed about a kernel, when a third swooped down and carried it off. (Zaïre)

Some proverbs provoke a laugh at the foibles of all people:

> One who recovers from sickness forgets about God. (Ethiopia)

> A silly daughter teaches her mother how to bear children. (Ethiopia)

Some understand the depths of human love:

> Let your love be like misty rain, coming softly but flooding the river. (Malagasy)

> Talking with one another is loving one another. (Kenya)

THE STORY AND MYTH

Because African languages were learned orally, and were seldom written down, myths and stories passed from generation to generation were the sources of history and legend. Revered storytellers recite their lore to children: stories of how the earth was formed, how the mountains grew, why the soles of a black person's feet are light, or why the lion is king.

As social change accelerates in Africa, the myths and legends also change. One legend from Kenya shows how white settlers were viewed:

How Mighty Is the White Man

After God had made men, the first ancestor of the Europeans tried to imitate him and to create a man too. And so he did. He built many men who looked exactly as they should, on the outside. But at the end, when he tried to make their hearts beat, he did not succeed. He had to give up. Therefore, unto this day, people say the white man is very mighty. He can do everything, even build people. If only he could make their hearts beat![16]

THE NEW LITERATURE OF PROTEST

Beyond the proverbs and legends, the new African writers have developed a rich treasury of prose and poetry, produced by the educated elite who expressed themselves in Arabic, Yoruba, Amharic, Swahili, and other African languages as well as in English, French, and Portuguese. First came a cry of protest against the colonists. In English-speaking Africa, this protest was a political one against the cruelty of the colonists. In French-speaking Africa, however, where selected Africans were to be citizens of France and where the educated were trained to become "Black Frenchmen," the cry was more against the destruction of African culture and heritage.

Chinua Achebe of Nigeria is what one American literary critic has called, "quite simply, one of the best novelists alive." In his novel, *Things Fall Apart,* he traces the coming of the white man and the consequent breakdown of many customs in the Nigerian village. At the end of the novel, Okonkwo, the main character, attempts to lead his friends in a rejection of the missionary, the church, and the colonial government. He organizes a meeting of villagers. When a colonial official, the District Commissioner, sends his Nigerian messenger in colonial uniform to break up the meeting, Okonkwo, in a fit of anger, kills the messenger.

> When the District Commissioner arrived at Okonkwo's compound at the head of an armed band of soldiers and court messengers he found a small crowd of men sitting wearily in the obi. . . . "Which among you is called Okonkwo?" he asked through his interpreter. "He is not here," replied Obierika.
> "Where is he?"

"He is not here!"

The Commissioner became angry and red in the face. . . .

"We can take you where he is, and perhaps your men will help us. . . ."

The Commissioner and his men followed, their firearms held at ready. . . . Then they came to the tree from which Okonkwo's body was dangling, and they stopped dead.

[One of the villagers says,] "Perhaps, your men can help us bring him down and bury him. . . ."

The District Commissioner changed instantaneously. The resolute administrator in him gave way to the student of primitive customs. "Why can't you take him down yourselves?" he asked.

"It is against our custom," said one of the men. Obierika, who had been gazing steadily at his friend's dangling body, turned suddenly to the District's Commissioner and said ferociously, "That man was one of the greatest men in Umofia. You drove him to kill himself; and now he will be buried like a dog. . . ."

He could not say any more. His voice trembled and choked his words.

"Shut up" shouted one of the messengers. . . .

The Commissioner went away. . . . In the many years in which he had toiled to bring civilization to different parts of Africa, he had learned a number of things. One of them was that a District Commissioner must never attend to such undignified details as cutting a hanged man from the tree. Such attention would give the natives a poor opinion of him. In the book which he planned to write he would stress that point. As he walked back to the court he thought about that book. Every day brought him new material. The story of this man who had killed a messenger and hanged himself would make interesting reading. One could almost write a whole chapter on him. Perhaps not a whole chapter but a reasonable paragraph, at any rate. There was so much else to include, and one must be firm in cutting out details. He had already chosen the title of the book after much thought *The Pacification of the Primitive Tribes of the Lower Niger.*[17]

In the 1950s, in French-speaking Africa, the protest was against the loss of "African-ness." The man who was most forceful in arguing for the uniqueness of the African was Leopold Senghor. He characterized the African genius as "Negritude."

> No, negritude . . . is neither racialism nor self-nega-tion . . . it is rooting oneself in oneself, and self-confirmation: confirmation of one's *being.* Negritude is nothing more or less than what some English-speaking Africans have called *African personality.* It is no different from the "black personality" discovered and proclaimed by the American New Negro movement. As the American poet, Langston Hughes wrote after the first world war: "We, the creators of the new generation, want to give expression to our *black personality* without shame or fear. . . . We know we are handsome. Ugly as well. The drums weep and the drums laugh. . . .
>
> What, then is negritude? It is . . . *the sum of the cultural values of the black world;* that is, a certain active presence in the world, or better, in the universe . . . it is essentially relations with others, an opening out to the world, contact and participation with others. Because of what it is, negritude is necessary in the world today; it is a humanism of the twentieth century.[18]

Some of these young writers in the new Africa were experiencing a love of homeland, a sense of identification with their illiterate brothers who remained in the villages, and a sense of insult at the racial discrimination that many found in the streets of Philadelphia, New York, London, and Paris. Wole Soyinka, a Nigerian dramatist, worked in London with the Royal Court Theatre. From his British experience he wrote the poem, "Telephone Conversation":

> The price seemed reasonable, location
> Indifferent. The landlady swore she lived
> Off premises. Nothing remained
> But self-confession. "Madam," I warned
> "I hate a wasted journey—I am African."
> Silence. Silenced transmission of
> Pressurized good-breeding. Voice, when it came,
> Lipstick coated, long gold-rolled
> Cigarette-holder pipped. Caught I was, foully,
> "HOW DARK?" . . . I had not misheard . . . "ARE
>   YOU LIGHT
> OR VERY DARK?" . . . It *was* real! Shamed
> By ill-mannered silence, surrender
> Pushed dumbfounded to beg simplification.
> Considerate she was, varying the emphasis—
> "ARE YOU DARK? OR VERY LIGHT?"
> Revelation came.
> "You mean—like plain or milk chocolate?"
> Her assent was clinical, crushing in its light.
> Impersonality . . .
> I chose
> "Madam," I pleaded, "wouldn't you rather
> see for yourself?"[19]

THE LITERATURE OF SELF-IDENTIFICATION

Beyond protest, African writers focused on the glories and foibles of common African life, a life in rapid change, with conflict between old and new. A Ugandan poet, Okot p'Bitek, who studied in Britain, wrote the "Song of Lawino." In the form of the lament of a scorned wife, it is in fact the lament of a whole people:

> . . . My husband pours scorn
> On Black People,
> He behaves like a hen
> That eats its own eggs,

A hen that should be imprisoned under
   a basket. . . .
He says Black People are Primitive
And their ways are utterly harmful
Their dances are mortal sins
They are ignorant, poor and diseased!
Ocol says he is a modern man
A progressive and civilized man,
He says he has read extensively and widely
And he can no longer live with a thing like me
Who cannot distinguish between good and bad,
He says I am just a village woman,
I am of the old type,
And no longer attractive,
He says I am blocking his progress. . . .
   Listen Ocol, my old friend,
The ways of your ancestors
Are good,
Their customs are solid
And not hollow,
They are not thin, not easily breakable,
They cannot be blown away
By the winds
Because their roots reach deep into the soil.
I do not understand
The ways of foreigners
But I do not despise their customs.
Why should you despise yours? . . .[20]

THE LITERATURE OF CRITICISM

The themes of protest continue today especially in the
writing of the black exiles of white-controlled South Africa.
In writing of men like Es'kia Mphalele they call for African
political rule and for identification with the African heritage.
In independent Africa, however, the most common themes
are criticism of favoritism, of self-interested politicians, and
of other wealthy elites.

Chinua Achebe writes about the self-interestedness of the university students in his novel, *A Man of the People,* in which the young student reflects on his ambitions:

> I had gone to the University with the clear intention of coming out again after three years as a full member of the privileged class whose symbol was the car. So much did I think of it in fact that, as early as my second year, I had gone and taken out a driver's license and even made a mental note of the make of car I would buy. . . . But in my final year I had passed through a crisis brought on partly by my radical Irish lecturer in history and partly by someone who five years earlier had been by all accounts a fire-eating president of our Students' Union. He was now an ice-cream eating Permanent Secretary in the Ministry of Labour and Production and had not only become one of the wealthiest and most corrupt landlords in Bori but was reported in the Press as saying that trade union leaders should be put in detention. He became for us a classic example of the corroding effect of privilege. Many of us vowed then never to be corrupted by bourgeois privileges of which the car was the most visible symbol of our country. . . .[21]

POETRY FOR THE MASSES: AFRICAN'S NEW MUSIC

Illiteracy remains high, and many of the common people find in music, on the radio, and in small bars, an expression of their feelings of love, loneliness, and life's adventures.

Village songs in one's home language remain popular. Hymns and religious music have a large audience.

The songs of the 1950s were love songs and laments. The refrain of one migrant worker's lament was:

> I shall die where I wander
> O Mother, O Mother
> I shall die where I wander.[22]

On the Zambian Copperbelt, one migrant worker commented about that song:

> I like this song because I come from far away to work
> for money. Now I do not think about returning home,
> and I have found my home in this place. While seeking
> a fortune here, I may die. I feel that I shall die far from
> my home since I am growing old now.[23]

Other songs tell the stories of the backward ways of a village wife, of the waywardness of a husband, of a girl who will not look at the singer, of true love found or lost—much like popular music everywhere.

Among the younger people there is a new thrust—a cosmopolitan music for all Africa. In the small rural villages, one may hear the melodies of Afro-American soul, disco, and reggae music. There is a growing identification with Afro-American musicians, many of whom have toured Africa.

Sweeping through Africa today, from the Gambia to Lesotho, is a popular new electric guitar sound called "Congo" or "Lumba" music. In southern Africa it is replacing the penny-whistle *kwela* (kwey' luh) and *phatha-phatha* (pah'-ta, pah'-ta) known in the United States through the songs of Miriam Makeba. In West Africa it is gaining in popularity over the predominant high-life, the swinging shuffle-dance of Nigeria and Ghana. This new Congo music was called "rumba" in the 1950s, reflecting the Latin American rhythms and instruments that had been copied from Afro-Cuban musicians.

More recently, the African bands have been imitating the music of Aretha Franklin, James Brown, and other Afro-American soul musicians, as well as Bob Marley and other Caribbean reggae artists, incorporating Latin American and African drums, shakers, and other rhythm instruments with the electric guitar. This music is truly a music of the new Africa. It responds to the changes of the day. New songs are written at election time and during national crises. A new dance was invented by a Congolese band in 1969. It imitated the slow-motion movement of Neil Armstrong's moon-walk and was named "The Apollo."

This glimpse into African music and literature is intended to encourage a more in-depth look at some of the authors, musicians, poets, and artists of Africa.

9

CONCLUSION

The continent of Africa is very diverse. It contains approximately one-fourth of the world's land mass and one-tenth of its people, who live in more than fifty nations and speak more than seven hundred languages—more nations and languages than any other continent. Therefore, any brief summary of this complex and vast continent must always be simplistic. Just as in the United States, in Africa there is great diversity of religion, race, values, types of work and wealth. We cannot make facile generalizations about African peoples and societies, and there certainly is no single type of "African personality," "African family," or "African voter." The American student seeking a greater depth of understanding of this continent, needs case-study materials of individual nations, societies, and families. The following list of resources about Africa provides the student with some suggested films and books to pursue this study.

In the years ahead, this continent will grow in political and economic importance, and its growth will affect the entire world, especially the United States. The links between Americans and Africans will grow in importance as trade and travel increase and as we come to know more about each other. Those developments will enrich both continents as we exchange raw materials, manufactured goods, philosophies, values, ideas, and music, and as the African and American people visit each other's worlds. Thus, the future holds promise for enriching our culture, our knowledge, our social diversity, our understanding of our common heritage, and our standards of living. It is important that we take each other more seriously. When we do, we shall realize that our isolation and our long period of ignorance of each other has harmed us both, for:

He who never visits, thinks his mother is the only cook.

(Ugandan and Ethiopian proverb)

AFRICAN COUNTRY NAMES BEFORE AND AFTER INDEPENDENCE AND DATE OF INDEPENDENCE

COUNTRY	DATE OF INDEPENDENCE	COLONIAL OR PRE-INDEPENDENCE NAME	COLONIAL POWER
Algeria	July 3, 1962	Algeria	France
Angola	Nov. 11, 1975	Angola	Portugal
Benin	Aug. 1, 1960	Dahomey (French West Africa)	France
Botswana	Sept. 30, 1966	Bechuanaland	Great Britain
Burundi	July 1, 1962	Ruanda-Urundi (also: German East Africa)	Great Britain, Germany
Cameroon	Oct. 1, 1961	French Cameroon (later part of British Cameroon) Kamerun (German)	France, Great Britain Germany
Canary Islands	—	—	Spain
Cape Verde	July 5, 1975	Cape Verde	Portugal
Central African Republic	Aug. 13, 1960	Oubangi-Chari (French Equatorial Africa)	France
Chad	Aug. 11, 1960	Chad (French Equatorial Africa)	France
Comoro Islands	June 6, 1975	Comoro Islands	France

(Note: one of the islands, Mayotte, has a special status with France, known as a *collective territoriale*.)

Congo	August 15, 1960	Congo (French Equatorial Africa)	France
Djibouti	June 27, 1977	French Territory of the Afars and Issas, French Somaliland	France
Egypt (Arab Republic of Egypt)	July 23, 1952 (revolution which led to founding of republic)	Egypt	Great Britain
Equatorial Guinea	Oct. 12, 1968	Spanish Guinea and Fernando Po	Spain
Ethiopia	—	(In 19th c. referred to as "Abyssinia")	—
Gabon	Aug. 17, 1960	Gabon (French Equatorial Africa)	France
Gambia	Feb. 18, 1965	Gambia	Great Britain
Ghana	March 6, 1957	Gold Coast, and British Togoland	Great Britain
Guinea	Oct. 2, 1958	Guinea (French West Africa)	France

COUNTRY	DATE OF INDEPENDENCE	COLONIAL OR PRE-INDEPENDENCE NAME	COLONIAL POWER
Guinea Bissau	Sept. 24, 1973	Portuguese Guinea	Portugal
Ivory Coast	Aug. 7, 1960	Ivory Coast (French West Africa)	France
Kenya	Dec. 12, 1963	Kenya (British East Africa)	Great Britain
Lesotho	Oct. 4, 1966	Basutoland	Great Britain
Liberia	July 26, 1847 (Declaration)	—	—
Libya	Dec. 24, 1951	—	Italy (1914: Britain occupied part of Libya)
Madagascar	June 26, 1960	Madagascar	France
Malawi	July 6, 1964	Nyasaland	Great Britain
Mali	Sept. 22, 1960	French Sudan (French West Africa)	France
Mauritania	Nov. 28, 1960	Mauritania (French West Africa)	France
Mauritius	March 12, 1968	Mauritius	Great Britain, France
Morocco	March 2, 1956	French & Spanish Morocco, Ifni, Tangier Zone	France, Spain
Mozambique	June 25, 1975	Portuguese East Africa	Portugal
Namibia	—	(formerly South-west Africa)	Illegally controlled by South Africa, Germany
Niger	Aug. 3, 1960	Niger (French West Africa)	France
Nigeria	Oct. 1, 1960	Nigeria (part of Br. Cameroon added, 1961)	Great Britain
Reunion	—	—	*Department* of France
Rwanda	July 1, 1962	Ruanda-Urundi	Belgium
Sao Tome & Principe	July 12, 1975	Sao Tome, Principe	Portugal
Senegal	Aug. 20, 1960	Senegal (French West Africa)	France
Seychelles	June 28, 1976	Seychelles	Great Britain, France
Sierra Leone	April 27, 1961	Sierra Leone	Great Britain
Somalia	July 1, 1960	British Somaliland, and Italian Somaliland	Great Britain, Italy

COUNTRY	DATE OF INDEPENDENCE	COLONIAL OR PRE-INDEPENDENCE NAME	COLONIAL POWER
South Africa	Dec. 11, 1931 (white minority rule)	Union of South Africa	Great Britain
Sudan	Jan. 1, 1956	Anglo-Egyptian Sudan	Great Britain
Swaziland	Sept. 6, 1968	Swaziland	Great Britain
Tanzania	Dec. 9, 1961	—	
Tanzania	Dec. 9, 1961 (union, April 25, 1964)	Tanganyika & Zanibar, German East Africa	Great Britain, Germany
Togo	April 27, 1960	French Togoland (Fr. W. Af.) British Togoland	France, Great Great Britain Germany
Tunisia	March 20, 1956	Tunisia	France
Uganda	Oct. 9, 1962	Uganda	Great Britain
Upper Volta	Aug. 5, 1960	Upper Volta (French West Africa)	France
Zaïre	June 30, 1960	Belgian Congo	Belgium
Zambia	Oct. 24, 1964	Northern Rhodesia	Great Britain
Zimbabwe	April 18, 1980	Rhodesia, Southern Rhodesia	Great Britain (White minority gov't declared indep. 1965)
Saharan Arab Democratic Republic	—	Spanish Sahara Rio de Oro	Morocco claims SADR, after indep. from Spain

Compiled by Katherine Thuermer, Michigan State University

NOTES

(Chapter 1)

1. Richard Hall, *The High Price of Principles* (London: Hodder and Stoughton, Ltd., 1969).

2. Julius Nyerere, "World in Revolution," *Catholic Worker,* XXXVIII, Number 9 (December 1971).

3. Kenneth Kaunda (Speech delivered in Zambia, January 17, 1972).

(Chapter 3)

4. "South-South Option," *Third World Quarterly.*

Chapter 4)

5. *Times of Zambia* (June 10, 1967).

(Chapter 5)

6. Cheikh H. Kane, *Ambiguous Adventure* (New York: Walker & Co., 1962).

7. Melville J. Herskovits, *Human Factor in Changing Africa* (New York: A.A. Knopf, 1962), quoting A. Victor Murray, *The School in the Bush* (London: Frank Cass Ltd., 1929).

8. A. Victor Murray, *The School in the Bush* (London: Frank Cass Ltd., 1929).

(Chapter 6)

9. Kenneth Kaunda, *A Humanist in Africa* (London: Longmans, 1966).

10. *Ibid.*

(Chapter 7)

11. *Apartheid in Practice* (New York: United Nations Office of Public Information, 1971).

12. Helen Suzman, M.P., *House of Assembly Debates* (June 17, 1969).

13. Kenneth Kaunda, *Zambia Shall Be Free* (London: Heinemann, 1962).

14. Kaunda, *A Humanist in Africa.*

(Chapter 8)

15. Charlotte and Wolf Leslau, eds., *African Proverbs* (Mount Vernon, NY: Peter Pauper Press, 1962).

16. *Ibid.*

17. Chinua Achebe, *Things Fall Apart* (Greenwich, CT: Fawcett Premier Books, 1959).

18. Leopold S. Senghor, "Negritude: A Humanism of the Twentieth Century," in Wilfred Cartey and Martin Kilson, eds., *The African Reader: Independent Africa* (New York: Random House, 1970).

19. Gerald Moore and Ulli Beier, eds., *Modern Poetry from Africa* (New York: Penguin, 1963).

20. Okot p'Bitek, "Song of Lawino," (Nairobi, Kenya: East African Publishing House, 1966).

21. Chinua Achebe, reprinted from *A Man of the People,* by permission of the John Day Co., Inc. Copyright ©1966 by Chinua Achebe.

22. Hortense Powdermaker, *Coppertown* (New York: Harper and Row, 1962).

23. *Ibid.*

GLOSSARY

Acebe, Chingua   A Nigerian novelist, author of *Things Fall Apart.*

African National Congress (ANC)   The leading black political party in South Africa.

Amin, Idi   The now exiled dictator of Uganda.

Apartheid   "Separateness." The South African policy of segregating the races socially, legally, and politically.

Bantustans   South African "homelands," or separate states, to which blacks in that country are assigned as part of the policy of apartheid.

Bilharzia   A parasitic worm that infects people as they wade in shallow water, causing schistosomiasis and resulting in damage to the liver.

Black Congressional Caucus   A coalition of black United States senators formed in 1971 to make demands for the national interests of black Americans.

Brain-drain   A migration of educated or trained people from one area to another in search of higher salaries or a better life-style.

Chama Cha Mapinduzi (CCM)   The one legal party of Tanzania.

Freedom Charter   A document that calls for a unified South Africa based on racial equality. It was adopted in 1955 by the African National Congress, the South African Indian Congress, the South Africa Coloured People's Organization, and the Congress of Democrats.

Great Rift   A geographical fault formed during prehistoric times, which created a chain of valleys running the length of the continent. Much of Africa's mineral wealth was exposed by this rift.

Great Zimbabwe   Huge stone structures constructed in Zimbabwe in prehistoric times.

Gross National Product (GNP)   The sum of the values of all goods and services produced by a country's residents in any given year.

Haile Selassie   Emperor of Ethiopia 1930-1936 and 1941-1974.

Homelands   See Bantustans.

Hut tax   Instituted by the colonial governments in Africa, this measure required families to pay taxes on each building in the village.

Islam   A religious faith started in Arabia during the seventh century by the Prophet Muhammad and brought to Africa by Muslim traders.

Kaunda, Kenneth   President of Zambia and a prominent black leader in Africa.

Koran   The sacred text of Islam. Foundation of law, religion, culture, and politics.

Kwame Nkrumah   The first leader of Ghana.

Malaria   A disease carried by mosquitos. It is characterized by periodic attacks of fever and chills.

Monoculture   The cultivation of a single product to the exclusion of other uses of land; a one-crop economy.

Muslims   Followers of the Islamic faith.

Negritude   An awareness and pride in one's African heritage.

Nyerere, Julius   President of Tanzania.

Obote, Milton   The democratically-elected prime minister of Uganda who was deposed by Idi Amin.

Okot p'Bitek A Ugandan poet.

Organization of African Unity (OAU) An association of all the independent states of Africa (except South Africa) whose goal is to promote unity and solidarity among African nations.

Rhodes, Cecil British administrator and financier in South Africa.

Schistosomiasis A disease common in Africa which is caused by the parasitic bilharzia worm and results in blood loss and tissue damage.

Senghor, Leopold President of Senegal and an originator of the concept of "negritude."

Shaka A nineteenth century warrior-conqueror who lived among the South African Zulu.

Slash-and-burn agriculture A system of fertilizing the soil by cutting down and burning trees and bushes.

Sleeping sickness A serious disease prevalent in tropical Africa. Transmitted by the tsetse fly, it is marked by fever, tiredness, tremors, and loss of weight.

Southeast African People's Organization (SWAPO) An Angolan-based nationalist group that has been waging guerrilla warfare against the South African presence in Namibia since the 1960s.

Soyinka, Wole A Nigerian dramatist.

Subsistence agriculture A system of farming that provides food crops for the farmer's family without leaving any surplus for sale.

Tsetse fly An insect which transmits sleeping sickness to cattle and humans. It is usually found in the scrub tree and forest regions of Central Africa.

Ujamaa Tanzanian agricultural cooperatives.

Vorster, John Former prime minister of South Africa.

RESOURCES ON AFRICA

AFRICAN STUDIES CENTER OUTREACH PROGRAMS TO SCHOOLS AND COMMUNITY ORGANIZATIONS

Nine major university centers are funded by the United States Department of Education as National Resource Centers on African Language and Area Studies. These centers generally possess the largest faculties, libraries, research projects, and cadres of African and Africanist students in the nation. As a result, they have rich personnel, data, and documentary resources on which to draw. Each center has an Outreach Director designated to serve the needs of teachers and the general public. Most have annotated selective bibliographies for specific disciplines and grade levels. Some have lending libraries of print and non-print teaching materials for use within the state where the center is located.

Africa in the School and
  Community
Boston University
125 Bay State Road
Boston, MA 02215
(617) 353-3673

Center for African Studies
  Outreach Programs
University of Florida
Grinter Hall
Gainesville, FL 32611
(904) 392-2183

Outreach Program
African Studies and Research
  Program
Howard University
Washington, DC 20059
(202) 636-7648

African Studies Educational
  Resource Center
Michigan State University
100 Center for International
  Programs
East Lansing, MI 48823-1035
(517) 353-1700

African Studies Program
Northwestern University
Dartmouth Place
Evanston, IL 60201

African Education Project
Stanford University
200 Lou Henry Hoover Building
Stanford, CA 94305
(415) 497-1114

African Studies Program
University of Illinois
  at Urbana-Champaign
1208 W. California, Room 101
Urbana, IL 61801
(217) 333-6335
African Studies Program
  Outreach
Indiana University
Woodburn Hall
Bloomington, IN 47405
(812) 337-7587

African Studies Center
University of Wisconsin
Madison, WI 53706
(608) 263-2171
Outreach Coordinator
African Studies Program
University of California at
  Los Angeles
Los Angeles, CA 90024
(213) 825-3686

GENERAL REFERENCES AND BACKGROUND READING

Martin, Phyllis M. and O'Meara, Patrick, eds. *Africa.* Bloomington: Indiana University Press, 1977.
This volume provides an introduction to Africa from the
mainstream point of view of United States Africanist
scholars.

Africa South of the Sahara (Annual). Published by Europa Publications Ltd., 18 Bedford Sq., London.
This single volume reference work on Africa includes
background articles on history, politics, geography, industry,
religion, agriculture, languages, and economic development.
Part II describes regional organizations in Africa such as the
Economic Commission for Africa. Part III gives twenty to
thirty pages of detailed summaries of each nation.

Hall, Susan J. *Africa in U.S. Educational Materials.* New York
African American Institute, 1977.
A guide to evaluating materials on Africa, with teacher and
student bibliographies.

Bascom, William. *African Art in Cultural Perspective: An Introduction.* New York: Norton and Company.
Illustrated continent-wide catalogue of African societies and
types of art they produce, with examples.

Davidson, Basil. *African Genius.* Boston: Little, Brown and Co.,
    1970.
    This book provides an excellent overview to the last hundred
    years of African history, covering the colonial period to the
    present time. Davidson has also written extensively on the
    armed struggles for liberation in Africa.

Area Handbooks (example: *Area Handbook for Sierra
    Leone*). Washington D.C.: Government Printing Office,
    197b, DA PAM 550-180.
    These large volumes are of varying dates of issue, but provide
    a one-volume summary on most African nations under the
    following headlines: society, history, physical environment,
    population, ethnic groups and languages, family, living
    conditions, education, arts and culture, religion, politics,
    government, legal system, foreign relations, media, econ-
    omy, agriculture, labor, industry, trade, fiscal monetary
    systems, and national security/military issues. Many maps
    and illustrations are included.

Thompson, R.F. and Joseph Cornet. *The Four Moments of the
    Sun.* Washington D.C.: The National Gallery of Art, 1981.
    This unique book discusses and illustrates the African-
    African American links through customs, gestures, arts and
    crafts from Africa alive today in American culture. Empha-
    sis is put on the African influence on all of American culture,
    not only on African-American culture.

Global Studies: Africa (Annual). Jane Martin, Contributing
    Editor. Guilford: Dushkin Publishing Group, 1984.
    The volumes of the Global Studies series provide statistical
    information, country reports, regional essays, and articles
    from the world press. Revised annually for currency.

Fage, J.D. *A History of Africa.* New York: Knopf, 1979.
    Recommended general introductory history of the continent.

Davidson, Basil. *Let Freedom Come.* Boston: Brown, Little,
    and Co., 1970.
    This book provides an excellent overview to the last hundred
    years of African history, covering the colonial period to the
    present time. Davidson has also written extensively on the
    armed struggles for liberation in Africa.

Nketia, J.H. Kwabena. *The Music of Africa.* New York: W.W. Norton, 1974.

Photo-illustrated with bibliography, information on African languages, terms, song texts and music, listing of recordings; very comprehensive.

Bhati, Purnima Mehta. *Scholar's Guide to Washington, D.C. African Studies.* Washington, D.C.: Smithsonian Press, 1980.

This guide describes special collections on Africa in libraries and museums, and sources of information such as US government offices, embassies, cultural exchange programs and educational agencies relating to Africa.

Sub-Saharan Africa and the United States. United States Department of State, Publication 9112, Superintendent of Documents, Printing Office. Washington, D.C.: US Government Printing Office, 1980.

A concise, 46-page booklet giving a topical profile of the continent, accompanied by photographs and maps. Includes a special section on US-African relations, and an appendix with important statistical data from each country.

Wiley, Marylee, ed. "Teaching About Africa," in *Social Education,* Vol. 46, no. 7. Washington, D.C.: National Council for the Social Studies, 1982.

Recent social studies textbooks are critically reviewed and evaluated. Articles on "African Arts and the Social Studies" and "New Perspectives on African History" and several lesson ideas for teaching about Tanzania are valuable resources for teachers.

NEWS AND INFORMATION SERVICES

Africa News—Box 3851, Durham, North Carolina 27702.

This weekly news magazine on Africa is the best source of current news on Africa for use by teachers in the United States. It is an independent source to balance and correct the more superficial reporting found in popular weekly news magazines.

Africa Report—Transaction Inc., Box A, Rutgers University, New Brunswick, NJ 08903.

This monthly journal provides a good analysis of current affairs in Africa. Contains an up-to-date map of African countries.

Habari News and Information Service/African Bibliographic Center—P.O. Box 13096, Washington, D.C. 20009.

This center provides the *Current Bibliography on African Affairs* and the Habari weekly news service on current events in Africa.

Objective Justice—New York, UN Office of Public Information.

This quarterly journal provides essays on current issues in southern Africa and includes many non-American authors.

ORGANIZATIONS WITH SPECIALIZED KNOWLEDGE AND EXPERTISE

American Committee on Africa—198 Broadway, Room 402, New York, NY 10038 (202-962-1210).

This is the oldest American voluntary association focused on African issues. Occasional publications of ACOA are very concise and useful for teachers.

African-American Institute—833 United Nations Plaza, New York, NY 10017 (212-949-5666); Washington, D.C. (202-872-0521).

AAI publishes *Africa Report*, hosts a number of conferences, arranges charter flights to Africa, and organizes performances and exhibits in the African arts. Unfortunately, the Schools Service Division has been discontinued and teaching materials are no longer available.

International Defense and Aid Fund for Southern Africa— P.O. Box 17, Cambridge, MA 02138 (617-491-8343).

Publishes resources on South Africa—poster sets, photo essays, print materials. Excellent for classroom display.

National Public Radio—2025 M. Street, N.W., Washington, D.C. 20036.

NPR sells audio tapes of programs about Africa aired on NPR. Write for this current listing.

TransAfrica—Suite #200, 545 8th Street, S.E., Washington, D.C. 20003 (202-547-2550).
TransAfrica provides services and activities very similar to the Washington Office on Africa, however with an African-American perspective and focus. Interlinked closely with the Congressional Black Caucus, African American communities in several cities, and other Afro-American leaders in the nation, the organization provides a lobby on a range of issues concerning blacks in Africa, the Caribbean, Latin America, and the United States.

Washington Office on Africa—110 Maryland Avenue, N.E., Washington, D.C. 20002 (202-546-5961).
Organized originally with church and voluntary support to provide a critical lobby on African affairs in Washington, this organization offers a nongovernmental center of action on African affairs in Washington. Activities include publication of newsletters and pamphlets on current African issues in Washington, analysis of US government policy and activities in Africa, lobbying on bills before Congress, and reference services for persons interested in African issues in Washington.

TEACHING UNITS AND STUDENT MATERIALS

Hicks, E.P., and B. Beyer. *Africa Inquiry Maps and Teaching Guide.* Sunburst Communications, 1977.
This program includes twenty sets of fourteen see-through maps of Africa, masters for fifteen student learning activities, and a teaching guide.

Burke, Fred, (ed.) *Africa: Selected Readings.* Boston: Houghton Mifflin, 1969.
Primary and secondary sources on a variety of topics for high school students.

Crane, Louise. *African Games of Strategy.* Urbana: African Studies Program, University of Illinois, 1983.
This new publication features math games and activities for classroom use.

Kwamina-Poh, M., et al. *African History in Maps*. London: Longman, 1982.

This is an excellent detailed collection of maps to use in teaching the history and geography of Africa, the early settlements and kingdoms, colonial period, contemporary Africa.

Crane, Louise. *African Names: People and Places*. Urbana: African Studies Program, University of Illinois, 1982.

Unit on African naming practices with suggestions for interdisciplinary classroom activities, includes maps, pronunciation guide.

Machin, Noel. *African Poetry for Schools, Book 1 and 2*. London: Longman, 1978.

Photo-illustrated anthologies of poetry from the black diaspora, graded in difficulty with pupil and teacher notes, ideas for dramatization.

African Writers Series.

Heinemann Educational Books distributes over 250 titles by African poets, novelists, playwrights and scholars. Excellent for English and social studies classes.

Coloring Book on African Art. Santa Barbara: Bellerophon Books, 1981.

Curriculum Materials for Teachers. Urbana: African Studies Program, University of Illinois.

Annually updated collection of over one hundred short pieces for levels K-12, including country information sheets, maps, topical essays, games, music, stories, bibliographies, film guides. Indexed.

Nigeria in Change. London: Centre for World Development Education.

This excellent set of materials includes photo sets on women and children, health; slide sets on Nigeria today and traditional Nigeria-Oyo.

Winther, Barbara. *Plays from Folktales of Africa and Asia*. Boston: Plays, Inc., 1976.

Contains six plays based on African folktales, from West Africa, Ethiopia and Egypt.

Soyinka, Wole, ed. *Poems of Black Africa.* New York: Hill and Wang/Farrar Straus and Giroux, 1975.
Representative collection of poems from all over Africa, including some translated from African languages.

Senanu, K.E., and T. Vincent. *Selections of African Poetry.* London: Longman, 1976.
Each selection is introduced and annotated.

Clark, Leon E., ed. *Through African Eyes.* New York: CITE World Cultures Series Council on International and Public Affairs, 777 U.N. Plaza, Suite 9-H, New York, NY 10017.
These six volumes provide primary source materials for teaching about colonialism, nationalism, urbanization, etc. Lesson plans are available for each volume.

Courlander, Harold, ed. *A Treasury of African Folklore.* New York: Crown, 1975.
Comprehensive collection of African folk literature, including stories, riddles, proverbs.

Ojigbo, A. Odion, ed. *Young and Black in Africa.* Random House, 1971.
In this book, eight Africans reveal dramatic episodes from their own lives.

US DISTRIBUTORS OF FOREIGN PUBLISHERS

The following provide print materials published abroad, including books used in African schools. Write for catalogues and consult African Studies Center outreach staff for assistance in selecting titles appropriate to your needs.

African Imprint Library Services
Box 563
Falmouth, MA 02541
(617) 540-5378

Longman Inc.
19 W. 44th Street
New York, NY 10036

Heineman Educational Books Inc.
4 Front Street
Exeter, NH 03833

Longman publishes an excellent geography series with a survey of economics, agriculture, natural resources and geography of African nations.

ERIC Materials

Instructional Units available from ERIC Document Reproduction Services, P.O. Box 190, Arlington, VA 22210.

African Art and Culture for High School Students of Art (10th-12th grade). Illustrated.

Stumpff, Marcelle. *An African Curriculum Unit* (10th-12th grades World Civilization). 21 pages.

Crowder, M., et al. *Ancient Times: A Junior History for Africa.* London: Longman Group Ltd., 1977.
Color photo-illustrated, simply written and designed for 11-12-year-olds, this covers Africa from beginnings of civilization, Greek and Roman Empires, early African states.

Harkless, Necia, ed. *A Nigerian Notebook: Units and Resources for Teachers and Parents-Early Childhood and Elementary.* Center for Professional Development, University of Kentucky, 1980.
Includes resources and activities for language arts, recipes, songs, bibliographies. Available through ERIC.

Wilson, Angene, ed. *Nigeria: Teaching Plans and Materials for Secondary School Teachers and Students.* Center for Professional Development, University of Kentucky, 1980.
Comprehensive (169 pages) unit including Nigerian constitution, information on election process, sample newspapers and ads, maps, historical background, many suggestions for activities. Available through ERIC.

AUDIO VISUAL MATERIALS

Films, Slides and Tapes

Usually the best A-V materials about Africa are ones on specific countries, cities, artists or other topics, and *not* about the continent in general (e.g. the New York Times kit "Africa: Portrait of a Continent").

Africa on Film and Videotape: A Compendium of Reviews. East

Lansing: African Studies Center, Michigan State University, 1982.

This is the definitive directory to African film available in the United States including over 750 reviews of the film by African and Africanist specialists. Some video material is included. Films and videotapes are referenced in the index by topic, country, language, and society. Details are provided on the length, date, director/producers, details of content, distributors, and suitability for elementary, middle or senior high use. Each film is evaluated on a 1-5 ranking. It is interesting to note that most of the recommended films are not in school collections, and most of the films in the school collections are not recommended. This is an indispensable guide for teachers of African studies.

Africa: Focus on West Africa. BFA Educational Media. Four filmstrips; four cassettes.

This kit presents two Ghanaian craftsmen (textile maker and wood carver) and the life of a yam farmer in the Ivory Coast.

Africa: A New Look. New York: International Film Foundation, 1980.

27 minutes. Color. Overview of Africa today, focusing at end on South Africa. Rental from Visual Aids Service, University of Illinois at Urbana. Purchase from International Film Foundation.

Dumor, Cecilia. *African Story Telling.* East Lansing: Global Studies Center, College of Education, Michigan State University.

28 minute video cassette. Color. Ms. Dumor, a Ghanaian teacher, tells stories to American children and discusses how Ghanaian story telling techniques can improve children's prereading skills. This may be used for teacher inservice workshops and in classroom.

Amandla! Washington, D.C.: Washington Office on Africa Educational Fund.

An excellent complement to the film "Last Grave at Dimbaza." This slide set presents a history of the vigorous resistance by Africans to the increasing power and oppression by the whites. It covers one hundred years of resistance. (*See* "Last Grave at Dimabaza")

Colonialism: A Case Study, Namibia. New York: United Nations TV.
21 minutes. Color. Reviews the period of German conquest and African resistance and explains how Namibia became a League of Nations Mandate and a UN Trust Territory under South African occupation.

Discovering the Music of Africa. Bailey Film Associates.
22 minutes. Color. Three types of Ghanaian instruments are presented: rattles, bells and drums. The film serves as a basic introduction to West African music.

Ethiopia: A Way of Life. Troll Associates, 1977.
Two filmstrips and two cassettes: one on city life, one on farm life. Gives a good introduction to Ethiopia.

Brown, Barbara. *Forget Not Our Sisters.* Boston: Boston University, 1982.
This slide/tape set is an excellent introduction to South Africa, apartheid, role of Western corporations there, with special emphasis on the effect of the system on women. For rental, available from American Friends Service Committee, 2161 Massachusetts Avenue, Cambridge, MA 02140 (617-497-5273). For purchase, available from BCLSA, P.O. Box 8791, Boston, MA 02114, (617-522-2744).

Global Interdependence: An African Perspective, revised edition.
East Lansing: African Studies Center, Michigan State University, 1981.
28 minutes. This set of slides and tapes shows the links between the US and Africa: through people, music, art, trade and the women's movement. It shows many products which come from Africa to the US and teaches interdependence.

Global Village: Ghana and *Global Village: Kenya.* Westinghouse Learning Press, 1973.
Although these sets (two filmstrips, two cassettes and one guide) were published a decade ago, they are still better than some published more recently. Available from Social Studies

School Services, 10,000 Culver Blvd., P.O. Box 802, Department 12, Culver City, CA 90230-0802.

Harambee, Kenya! InterCultural Associates, 1978.
Four filmstrips; four cassettes. Available from Social Studies School Services (see above address). Good introduction to Kenya.

Kenya Trilogy: Films Incorporated, 1973.
White Man's Country—the story of colonial "British East Africa" now until independence. *Mau Mau*—describes the meaning of "Mau Mau" in Kenya and explains the meaning of "Mau Mau" as a political and military response to repression. *Kenyatta*—depicts the activities and life of Jomo Kenyatta.

Last Grave at Dimbaza. Morena Films.
58 minutes. Color. This film is the best single introduction to South African apartheid, the racially based social, political, and economic structure of South Africa (*See* "Amandla").

Schmidt, Gerhard. *South Africa Belongs to Us.* San Francisco: Southern Africa Media Center, 1980.
35 mm. Color. Interviews and closeups on five women in South Africa long involved in the liberation struggle, includes a secretly shot interview with liberation leader Winnie Mandela.

Tauw. New York: New Yorker Films, 1970.
27 minutes. Color. A day in the life of a twenty-year-old unemployed man of Dakar, Senegal. This film breaks stereotypes about Africa and provides a realistic view of life for the elite and the poor of urban Africa.

West Africa Today. Educational Activities Inc., 1978.
These four filmstrips cassettes are narrated by West Africans with music in the background. They give a good introduction to city and village life and to the arts and crafts of West Africa.

West Africa: Two Life Styles. Bailey Film Associates, 1970.
20 minutes. Color. Focuses on the daily routines of two people in the Ivory Coast—one a businesswoman, the other a

farmer. Excellent film to give constructive and accurate knowledge about urban and rural life.

Folktales on Film

Anansi the Spider. Texture Films, 1969.
> 10 minutes. Color. Adventures of Anansi, a folk hero of Ghana.

Atumpan: The Talking Drums of Ghana. UCLA, 1964.
> 42 minutes. This film depicts the creation of a drum, from the selection of the tree to the ceremonial use made of the drum. It is a highly detailed film not suitable for younger children.

Cow-Tail Switch. Learning Corporation of America, 1970.
> 8 minutes. Story of Ogaloussa the hunter who fails to return home. The moral of the story is that people are not really dead until they are forgotten.

Magic Tree. Texture Films, 1970.
> 10 minutes. Color. Folk tale about an unloved son who leaves home and finds a magic tree which changes his life.

Mapandangare: The Great Baboon. Sterling Educational Films, 1978.
> 10 minutes. Color. This film combines story telling with an introduction to musical instruments from Africa.

The Rug Maker: A Folktale of Africa. Learning Corporation of America, 1970.
> 9 minutes. Color. An East African folktale about Kamilo, a young man who becomes a rugmaker to please a young girl he wants to marry.

INDEX

Index